CONVINCE
LIKE
A
COUNSELOR

A Lawyer's Guide to Mastering
Persuasion, Charisma, and Influence

TOMER SOFER

Production by eBookPro Publishing
www.ebook-pro.com

CONVINCE LIKE A COUNSELOR
Tomer Sofer

Copyright ©2024 Tomer Sofer

Translation from Hebrew: Noam Heller
Editing: Nancy Alroy

Contact: soferlawoffice@gmail.com

ISBN 9798332555350

Contents

PART 3 — THE MESSAGE

Learn How to Influence Anyone

Throughout our lives, we bear a heavy sack filled with our dreams, ambitions, goals and countless desires we wish to fulfill. This sack can hold our biggest dreams, such as finding true love, landing a coveted job or launching a thriving business, as well as smaller desires such as taking a vacation with our spouse or getting help from a neighbor to assemble the new bookcase we just purchased.

The more dreams and goals and desires that we are able to extract from this sack over the course of our lifetime, the closer we will get to creating our own 'paradise,' our own 'heaven' — that place where are able to live a rewarding, pleasant and happy life.

But we are not alone in this world. We are surrounded by people who seek to fulfill their own desires and dreams, which may often be the opposite of ours. Therefore, the manner in which we go about trying to create our own heaven and achieve our own objectives will often require consent and approval from others.

This journey of ours means we need to become experts in the arts of persuasion and influence: to put ourselves in a position to succeed, to effectively convey our messages and ideas, to be able to affect people's opinions and get them to go along with our wishes and agree with our positions.

On the way to creating our own paradise we will traverse three different tracks and we must commit to upholding one key condition; should we regularly and blatantly fail to meet this condition, our paradise will turn to ruins and, instead, will become a sad and depressing place in which to live.

The first track we will follow is the longest and least straightforward of the three. Its length equals that of our entire lifetime. On this track we will undertake a fascinating journey to discover our personal uniqueness and strength which have no peer. In the course of this 'journey to paradise,' we shall see that every act of persuasion and influence, every success in realizing our dreams, begins within us — by tapping into our unique strengths. The deeper we go in our search for self-understanding, the more we discover about ourselves along the way, and the more that unique strength that burns within us will be manifested.

You wouldn't be surprised if I told you that most people are apprehensive about embarking on a lengthy quest and, therefore, right from the start of their journey, from the very first steps, they stop and then spend the rest of their lives sitting on the sidelines, essentially just awaiting the bell that signals the end of their journey on this earth. But, forging ahead on this challenging course is crucial if we genuinely want to discover how effective our powers of influence and persuasion can be, and how we can harness them in order to achieve our biggest dreams and create a happier and more rewarding life for ourselves.

The second track we will follow over the course of our life is shorter and less intensive than the first one. On this track, we will learn how to relate to the people around us with a power we didn't know we had, to create chemistry and a strong connection with them on a subconscious level, and induce them to respect and like us without even being aware of it. As we become more skilled in understanding people and improve our ability to connect with them, we will find that we succeed, as if by the wave of a magic wand, in eliciting from them the response that we seek to help us to create our own heaven.

The third track is the shortest, yet also the most enjoyable and easiest to implement. This is the track on which we will learn practical advice, strategies and rules for being able to influence others quickly and directly. On this track, we need no spiritual or philosophical aspects such as those related to discovering our uniqueness or creating a deep connection with people. On this track, we will learn 'the language of heaven' — a unique language in which we will understand how to use empowering words, convincing arguments and intriguing stories in order to quickly attain our desires, dreams and goals by the way we affect the people around us. Often, we will find that a captivating story, precise arguments, or the right choice of words can help us get people to agree to our requests easily and quickly, regardless of our special inner strength or the chemistry we have with people. Frankly, most of the courses and workshops I know of in the field of influence and persuasion focus primarily on this track, because it is considered the most practical and can produce relatively fast results. But it is important to understand that the effectiveness of this track is limited when it comes to our overall ability to influence people; when we are talking about achieving our biggest dreams and goals in life — the first two tracks we mentioned are critical. We cannot achieve our goals without them.

In order to create our own heaven, there is one crucial condition that we must uphold. If we knowingly and repeatedly fail to meet this condition, we will be 'expelled' from paradise and a satisfying life will recede from our reach. All denizens of paradise are responsible for one another. In order to create our own paradise, we must help others to create theirs as well. It is not possible to create our own heaven by trampling upon and destroying the heaven of the people around us, certainly not in the long run or as a life philosophy. The more we work to achieve our dreams and desires based upon a central idea of giving to others and having a powerful desire to help others, the more stable, impressive and durable the structures we build in our heaven will be. The more our attitude is focused on extending a helping hand to others and the more we put others at the center, the more we will achieve our desires and the easier we will build our own (and others') heaven.

At first, this rule may sound a bit strange and illogical. All our lives we've been taught that in order to survive and obtain more, we need to think of ourselves and not of others. A misguided rule has been drummed into us, one that says: Either I profit, or the other guy profits. This mistaken rule tells us that in order to survive and achieve what we want in life, we must be more cunning and silver-tongued than anyone else, we must always be striving to outmaneuver them. Unfortunately, a majority of people are motivated by this approach, with predictable results: constant frustration that they are not creating their vision of heaven. In this book, I will try to convince you that there is another approach to take if you wish to influence others; an approach that will yield much greater benefits and successes without having to trample anyone else in the process.

I decided to write this book not because I have many years of experience as a lawyer who appears in court and argues cases for a living, or because I conduct negotiations with people on a daily basis. Nor is it because of my degrees in business administration and law, or the countless courses and enrichment programs I have participated in, or the long list of books I have read over the years on the subject of influence and persuasion. Without a doubt, all of these things have helped to sharpen my professional skills in the field of persuasion and equip me with many important insights, the bulk of which are presented in this book. However, the book you now hold in your hands was mainly written because I am just an ordinary person who, like you, found myself on this fascinating journey called life, and have striven to uncover my unique personal strengths, to connect to my fellow human beings and to tell my individual story in order to influence others and bring my (and their) heaven to fruition.

An Introduction to Creating the Magic of Heaven

From the moment we come into this world, wailing and seeking out our mother's milk, until the moment we draw our last breath, we are constantly striving to fulfill more and more dreams and desires. Even when we leave this world, and are dead and buried, we leave behind a will in which we ask our loved ones to carry out our last wishes.

Far too many people are walking around on this earth depressed and miserable. Hardly anything they yearn for comes to fruition. Almost everything they want remains out of reach. Far too many people depend on tranquilizers and painkillers to dull the oppressive feeling that their life is not satisfying. Day by day, they drag themselves along in despair, step after step, towards their foregone end, without ever having achieved what they really wanted, without having realized a single dream of any substance or having devoted themselves to a single lofty purpose. At the same time, walking among us are people who do feel a sense of satisfaction, who each day are at work on constructing their own heaven. Yet so many others are living their lives in misery and feeling ostracized and shut out of heaven.

In this book, together we will take the first steps that must be taken in order to create your (and others') heaven, and I shall furnish you with a practical roadmap. It will be up to you to take the rest of the steps yourselves. No one else can do this important work for you.

What would your idea of heaven consist of? Some might say that, for them, heaven is a situation in which they have a happy and fulfilling relationship or marriage, in which they are prospering at work, in which their children are happy and healthy and respectful. It could be having a feeling of love and respect for yourself. You're healthy and vital, you have friends who love you and want to spend time with you. You make enough money to live the life you've chosen without worries and without needing anyone else's help. You are expanding your knowledge and horizons in a wide range of areas. You have a rich emotional, spiritual and intellectual world. You have pleasurable hobbies like playing the piano or going on cycling trips, and you are a moral person who cares about the environment and does what you can to preserve it. Others might say that their heaven looks somewhat different. They may have more or fewer dreams they wish to attain.

How do you picture heaven?

The desire to persuade and influence is the fuel that propels the thoughts and actions that lead to the realization of dreams and goals. Just as a car cannot drive even one meter without fuel, we too will not achieve anything at all in our entire life if we have no grasp of the art of persuasion and influence; just as a good driver is one who drives the car automatically without consciously thinking about all the actions that go into driving, the person who wants to fulfill his ambitions and dreams must use his persuasive abilities in an automatic, subconscious manner, without thinking about it too much.

Every peace agreement ever signed between countries was signed because politicians became convinced that this was the right step to take; wars begin and end because leaders are convinced that this is the correct path; presidents and heads of state are elected because they have successfully made their case to the people and persuaded the public that they are worthy of the position.

But major world events are not the only things that rely upon influencing and persuasion. The lives of each and every one of us are affected by our persuasive capabilities, from the moment we get up in the morning until the moment we go to bed at night. The newborn infant cries at night and persuades his mother to get out of bed and nurse him; the mother who had a sleepless night persuades her partner to make coffee and breakfast for her; on a trip to the shopping mall, the husband persuades the salesman to give him a discount on a shirt from the new collection; the salesman persuades his boss to give him a raise; the boss persuades his son to do his homework; and the boy persuades himself to work harder in school in order to be accepted to a prestigious school next year. Each of us is persuading and being persuaded all day long throughout our lives.

Notice that, at practically every moment in our lives, like sitting ducks, we are exposed to thousands of messages and ideas that are fired at us all day long from companies and corporations and a whole host of sources that are trying to persuade us what to eat, what to wear, what computer to buy, what destination to travel to, what to think, what to believe in, what to love, what to prefer, what kind of lifestyle is best for us, how we should live our lives, what will make us feel happier and more beautiful, and countless more messages that we are barraged with on the radio, in the papers, on television, online, on billboards and all kinds of advertising, from friends and acquaintances — all wanting us to accept their idea and act accordingly.

Similar to an onion, people are wrapped in many layers of desires, ideas and messages absorbed from other people and other entities that tell them how they ought to live their lives, that tell them what is good and bad for them. This situation led me to wonder what would happen if we were to remove all the layers of messages and ideas and desires that other people and those with a vested interest have been placing upon us since day one. What, then, would we really want? What, then, would our goals and dreams? And how would all this affect our lives and our persuasive capability? The answers to these questions will directly affect the empowerment of our persuasive ability and the attainment of our life's dreams and goals.

The art of persuasion and making a convincing case is the art of life. Every person needs to be conversant in it if he or she wants to live a life that its rewarding and vital. A carpenter uses his tools — hammer, nails, saw, pliers, and so on — to build cabinets and tables and kitchens. The tools that we will use to help us influence and persuade people include logical arguments, stories, words, tone of voice, body language and, above all: our uniqueness and the way we connect with other people.

This book essentially presents one big argument — my argument for how each one of us can create our own heaven by achieving our dreams and desires while helping the people with whom we come in contact to create their own heaven. The case I am making here is built upon my own experience — in my personal life with my wife and children, in the courtroom, in managing negotiations, in encounters with clients and friends, in long hours of solitary reflection, from observations of people, from reading books, from lectures, from conversations with wise, insightful people, and from all of my experiences in my life's journey so far.

In reading this book, I invite you to join me on a shared journey toward persuasion in which I will offer my insights and advice on how to create your own heaven and how to persuade and influence others in order to achieve your heart's desire. There may certainly be claims or explanations in the book with which you disagree. We may not always see things eye to eye. One of this book's goals is to prompt you to think of other insights or arguments that are unique to you and your personal life journey. Disagreement between us is welcome. It, too, is something that will empower you, because you, too, have your journey and your insights that you wish to share as a gift with others. Ultimately, you will know that you are following the right roadmap if you see that you are creating your own (and others') heaven.

PART 1

I

Gifts on the Road to Heaven

I recently signed up for an online lecture and paid a small fee. The audience was promised innovative, valuable information on a topic I cared about, and the lecturer himself was a renowned specialist in his field who assured us we would get our money's worth. Naturally, I had high hopes, as did many others. But, as it turned out, the higher the expectation, the greater the disappointment. The man on stage was too busy praising himself and didn't bother giving any novel insights. Instead of discussing innovative topics, he focused his energy on aggressively selling his precious courses. Needless to say, most of the people who took part were terribly disappointed over wasting their evening on such vanity.

To significantly improve our persuasion and influencing skills, we need to act as if we are granting others a gift — our gift. Instead of manipulating people into doing what we want, we should first help them get what they want.

In line with the 'Gift Approach,' we'll treat those around us in the same manner we would like to be treated — no manipulation, no trickery, no lies. Only integrity, sincerity, and love. Put simply, let the generosity in you ignite the spark of generosity in others.

It is said in the Book of Proverbs: "As in water face answereth to face, so the heart of man to man." In other words, just as water reflects the face, so our heart is reflected in the heart of the other. Our manner of approaching others determines how others will approach us. If we gift others — we will be gifted in return.

Even if your audience isn't inclined to buy your idea or turns down the product you're offering — it's for the better. Perhaps, at this moment in time, your client can not accept your gift, and that's okay. One must respect that. Never use aggression when it comes to persuasion. On the contrary, an understanding smile is the best way to go about it. If we stick to the 'Gift Approach,' people will appreciate our kindness and may return to us in the future, when the timing is right. At the very least, they may pass the word.

Multiple Paths to Heaven

Persuasion is the process of influencing another's behavior or attitude to achieve a desired outcome. For example, to get a raise, one must present satisfactory arguments to their boss. If the message conveyed is convincing enough, their paycheck will see a nice boost.

But persuasion isn't exercised solely through logical reasoning or elaborate arguments. There are various ways for us to fulfill our wishes: a show of stubbornness, kindness, empathy, cooperation, silence, and tears are just a few examples.

As a young, inexperienced lawyer at the start of his career, I viewed every court hearing as a power struggle in which only the strong survive. Eat or get eaten. I believed that the boisterous act of flailing one's hands in the air while cursing was the best way to be noticed. Of course, I was completely wrong. One day, shortly after I got married, I called my wife from the office to cancel our plans for the evening: "I won't be able to take you out to dinner, I'm overloaded with work." Truth be told, that wasn't the case. I could have left the office earlier but, as a newly-wed man, I was fixed on showing my wife that, despite our new status, I still played by my rules. My wife replied with an air of puzzling coolness. She said she respected my decision and would be waiting for me at home. Her response left me bewildered. I was sure she'd flip out for bailing at the last minute. Equipped with all the right arguments, I was ready to launch them, just like I did in court. However, my wife didn't bat an eyelid. Instead, she replied to my childish behavior with the utmost respect and care. In the face of this odd reaction, I was caught completely off guard. I felt like an idiot, like a child splayed on the floor of a toy shop begging their mommy for a toy. A few minutes later, I called my wife to let her know I'd be home tonight as planned.

My wife managed to get what she wanted without using any sophisticated arguments. She could have given me a hard time, and she had fair reason to do so. But it was how she kept her cool that affected me more than anything else. It was her silence that brought me home.

The process of persuasion never calls for subduing or humiliating the other person. There's no need to get them to drop on their knees, white flag in hand, crying bitter tears as they succumb to the pressure. No one appreciates that.

Using aggression to influence others doesn't work, at least not in the long run. It's important to acknowledge this as you venture through the first few chapters of this book as this paradigm shift will allow you to achieve your goals, ultimately culminating in the paradise you long for.

We'll come to realize that, on most occasions, love is the absolute best argument we have. It's a deadly weapon, stashed deep in our arsenal, with the power of moving people. As a lawyer, it took me a while to understand that love and respect can open almost every door we believe to be closed.

Indian leader Mahatma Gandhi triumphed over the British Empire without a trace of violence. Using only himself as a role model of peace and tolerance, he achieved his goal of leading India to freedom.

On our path to paradise, we'll discover there are many ways to influence others that don't include contentious arguments or aggressive actions. Using force or humiliating others won't take us very far. Love and respect, however, are forces that know no boundaries.

Heaven — Not Just for the Elite

While talking to others, I've learned something unfortunate — most people believe that influencing others is a trait belonging to the elite. As if only people at the top of the societal hierarchy — celebrities, successful businesspeople, and politicians — harness this magical force called persuasion. The 'regular' people, on the other hand, just don't have it. "Either you have it or you don't," is a sentence I often hear. They back this up by name-dropping a host of charismatic and influential people — all at the top of the hierarchy with an envy-provoking resume to their name — and compare them to the rest of the stale, humdrum members of society.

I've heard time and time again people stating that they're not cut out for persuading others, that they don't have the charisma or wit to sell anything to anyone. For them, it's set in stone — they just weren't born with 'it.'

At times, people will justify their pessimistic outlook by claiming that they've already given it a try before and have failed miserably. Absurdly enough, these same people can do a pretty good job of convincing us that they can't convince others. Just imagine the heights they'd reach if they were to put that same passion and motivation into arguments pertaining to other topics.

My argument is clear — each and every one of us has the power to persuade. It's as naturally ingrained in humans as barking is to dogs. Humans were born to move others; to lay out beliefs with passion and mold their lives. The older we get, though, the easier it is to lose track of the passion, ambition, and confidence that easily poured out of us as kids. Afflicted by life's hardships, most people have lost the will to stand up for their beliefs or, rather, no longer have the intellectual aptitude to come up with original claims. They're left wide-eyed, like a rabbit caught in the headlights, unable to fend for themselves.

Everyone is capable of persuading anyone, anytime, anywhere. One doesn't need to be a sharp-mouthed politician, a millionaire or a celebrity. As long as we use our wits and stick to authenticity over blind conformity — our inspiration and influence on others will be limitless.

Is it Better to Convince or Impress?

A few years ago at a court hearing, I sat in the gallery and observed the lawyers presenting their arguments to the judge. One of the lawyers seemed particularly impressive, donning an expensive suit and silver hair, a token of his seniority in the court of justice.

Courteously yet firmly, the lawyer asked the judge to allow a stream of funds, currently seized by the bank, to flow into his client's account. He went into great detail, mapping out his argument by using primary legal sources, eventually tying every bit of thread together to reach a conclusive statement. The opposing lawyer, representing the bank's side of the story, stubbornly refused to release the confiscated funds and argued before the judge that these funds, by law, shouldn't be released for many different reasons. Upon hearing both arguments, the judge decided to side with the bank.

Suddenly, the lawyer's client asked the judge for permission to say a few words. She was in her late 50s, dressed in drabby clothes, no makeup, her back slightly crouched. Even though the judge lacked the desire to hear more, she allowed the client to speak out of sheer politeness.

With an honest display of tears, the client shared her dire situation — her three young grandkids were under her care as their troubled mother was locked away in rehab. The father had walked out on the family ages ago and never once paid child support. The word's tumbled out of the client's mouth, with an air so hopeless it struck everyone in court. She described the empty fridge, the electricity being turned off, and the insufferable winter cold. These abandoned kids had nothing to hold on to but the goodwill of family and friends.

As she bared her soul, everyone, including the judge, appeared to be under a spell. In all of my years as a lawyer, I'd never seen any of my colleagues speak in such a sincere, captivating tone. The judge, evidently moved by this woman's heartbreaking testimony, changed her mind and allowed the retrieval of the funds in question. As for the lawyer representing the bank, he didn't have the heart to object to it either.

The woman's lawyer was, undoubtedly, more well-versed and charismatic, using dramatic body language and words as weapons. However, he failed to get his client the money she desperately needed. It was the client herself, a grandmother who hadn't gone to law school nor taken any fancy lessons in public speaking, who won the trial. Without any sophisticated maneuvers, she used her raw emotion to move the judge in her direction.

When people lose in arguments, it's not because they lack ingenious answers or can't articulate themselves properly. They lose by not being authentic.

What is Holding Us Back?

For the most part, people aren't too eager to take matters into their own hands, nor fight for what they care about. Our generation has been plagued by the numbing effect of screens, impairing our ability to connect, even with our loved ones. People struggle to share bits of their lives — like the lyrics of a song they wrote or how they genuinely feel. We find it hard to relax or allow a sincere, child-like laugh to bubble up in our bellies for no apparent reason. We're fixed in our ways, enclosed in our shells, shielding ourselves from reality like frightened turtles hiding from a predator.

If you place two little kids in a playground you'll have them running around together in no time, despite the awkward notion that they were strangers a second before.

However, somewhere along the trajectory of our adulthood, we've been robbed of that raw energy. We've nestled ourselves deep in the throes of our comfort zones, creating a blockade so firm we can no longer get out. We're hiding from the snarky comment that our elementary school teacher shot at us when we gave the wrong answer. We're hiding from the boisterous, disdainful laughter of our schoolmates when we confessed to having a crush. We're hiding from the boundless display of cynical comments, degrading remarks, rolls of the eyes, and arrogant chuckles expressed by those closest to us, intentionally or otherwise. The crossfire of painful words tossed at us throughout our lives has hardened our protective layers so much so that we've lost all will to peek outward.

Therefore, people prefer to keep silent about their situations without any attempt to prove their worth.

If we could magically read these people's minds —

their deepest, darkest secrets haunting their subconscious — we'd discover an unfortunate pattern of detrimental thoughts and emotions, far beyond their scope of awareness. Like a rollercoaster at full speed, our toxic thought patterns hoist us along as we shriek in fear, blinded by the blur of the moment. We're left stunned, spiraling in misery, cast away from our own, private Heaven.

These toxic thoughts include

"How can I be honest with friends and family? They might get angry. I don't deal well with confrontation. It's best I shut up and keep my passions and opinions to myself."

"How can I persuade people I don't know? What if I get on their nerves? I hate hearing 'no' for an answer; it's a horrible word that makes me shrivel. It's best I shut up and keep my thoughts to myself."

"Will they laugh at me if I disagree? I'd better shut up, even if that means settling for something I don't want."

"What if I ask my boss for a raise? Will they fire me for being greedy? The holidays are coming, I don't want to end up jobless and miserable. I'd better shut up; anyway, the company hasn't been doing so well lately."

"Will my opinions upset my friends? I don't want to be left behind. I don't have that many friends anyhow."

"I'm not a salesperson... I don't know how to push my ideas forward. I also don't want to manipulate others just so I could get what I want."

These are just a few examples of the kinds of thoughts

flashing through our minds at dizzying speed, hibernating in the nooks and crannies of our brains only to spring at us at the worst of times.

This is why most of humanity appears to be trudging along with crouched backs and heads hanging lifelessly from their frail necks. They'd rather keep their thoughts to themselves and embrace other people's narratives instead of their own. The sad truth is that, because of this, most humans would rather keep their biggest, most burning desires on hold.

What is life, though, if we're not living as our true selves with our genuine ideas? Without forming meaningful, authentic relationships; without advancing, growing, spreading, and embracing love — are we actually living? What is life if we can't be vulnerable, if we can't, simply put, be ourselves?

Our limiting thoughts, attitudes and perceptions, which have grown right under our noses, are now overwhelming us as adults. They've become a monstrous force threatening to demolish the towers of our hopes and dreams. They're there not because someone has placed a gun to our heads, nor has an evil force injected us with this poisonous stream. Rather, they've crawled under our skin as worms because we haven't been aware enough to stop them, nor did we have the tools to approach them with calm. Our memories, to which we have granted a twisted interpretation — now have a hold on our lives, so tight they are crushing us.

Inadvertently, we have amassed a collection of scarring memories, like the pang we felt in our chest in the first grade when the whole class burst into laughter after we gave a wrong answer. And perhaps, to make matters worse, the teacher shook her head and cynically snorted, "Stupidity knows no bounds. You've obviously not done your homework." At that painstaking moment, the humiliation etched itself into our skin, forcing us to believe we were, indeed, stupid, and that it was better to keep to ourselves rather than speak up. The seed, now planted, would sprout and dictate all of our actions. Years later, we'd end up as timid adults, trembling, with no backbone, controlled by our fears, enslaved by a demon whose roots could be traced back to the first grade.

Each belittling and self-deprecating thought has multiplied itself exponentially along the course of our lives and is now a heavy burden we carry, like a middle-aged man whose breathing has grown heavy, burdened by the extra pounds he has let creep on his waistline over the years. No wonder we don't feel worthy of persuading anyone of anything. Why let our true colors shine? Who would listen to our song anyway? There's no point in putting ourselves out there if we are going to be ridiculed by the world, right? Why risk hearing more "no's" in life? Why should we be humiliated, yet again, for thinking differently? Maybe it's best we keep quiet, forget our dreams, and give up the idea of heaven on Earth.

When a baby elephant first stumble into the circus, it is tied to a pole. Of course, the little creature attempts to break free of the chain but, lacking the strength, fails time after time. Alas, the little elephant gives into its situation, succumbing to the fact that it will never be free again. By the time it has grown into a full-fledged adult with enough force to storm through the circus tent it doesn't try to release itself from the pole anymore. The grown elephant believes it is still small and hopeless against the menacing stake. Sadly, this belief has become second nature.

Tragically, I can envision so many people tied to some imaginary pole, unable to create the life they want for themselves. They're conditioned by fear, insecurity, and other crippling beliefs.

The point of our journey is to strip ourselves of these debilitating illusions and adopt an empowering approach. Through enough reassurance we can inspire, persuade, move and, ultimately, help ourselves and others reach paradise.

No Room for Imposters

As time passes, people gradually cease to pay attention to their own unique traits and instead mimic others' characteristics, assuming that whatever worked for that guy will work for them too.

Today's populistic culture is constantly flashing the same message to us through various media outlets — if only you follow in this person's footsteps; if only you listen to this commercial or that political leader, you'd be happy.

These ideas are planted in our minds at every possible opportunity. If only we use this perfume, wear these shoes, these clothes, drive this car, or eat this cereal with the face of this basketball player on the box — we'll somehow become experts at shooting hoops.

Over the years we've been conditioned, right under

our noses, to be too compliant, passive, loyal to the system and, of course, to be hungry consumers. We've become predictable and are easily exploited by corporations, brands, and governments.

In nearly every station of our lives, from kindergarten to college, we've been taught to avoid confrontation. Never go against the grain. Become a part of society and accept its values. Don't push anyone's buttons and, most importantly, don't be a nuisance.

Parents, teachers, bosses, massive corporations, and the state — all benefit from our following their lead and adopting similar values.

Of course, by standing out, you'll make life more difficult for others. If you look back in time, however, history is full of people who made a change in the world, particularly because they refused to take the road less traveled.

Unbeknownst to us, we have become our society's puppets, soldiers of our parents, teachers, corporations, brands, friends, religious leaders, and every possible institution thirsty for our attention and obedience. We've become a product of other people's expectations rather than being our true selves.

No wonder people have begun to downgrade themselves, selling themselves short as if they were just another cog in the system with absolutely no unique or worthy qualities. People lack self-respect and a deep connection to those special quirks that make them who they are.

On the path to creating our own, personal paradise, we must strip ourselves from the veils and masks and phony façade we've devised under society's pressure. It's important to note why we've taken on such phoniness in the first place. If you observe your motives carefully, you'll notice that they come from a temporary craving, a desire to feel pleasure, if only for a while. We follow the dreams others sell us just so we can feel some satisfaction. But, in doing so, we become imposters, a sad imitation of someone else. And we all know that imitations are nothing more than a scam.

Imagine finding out that the stunning diamond you purchased at the jewelry store was, in fact, nothing more than simple glass. Chances are that your keen excitement over that possession will drop in an instant. Perhaps that's the reason few people get excited about their lives. How excited can you get from a hoax?

On the internet, a virtual world where most of us spend valuable hours surfing, we're bombarded by commercials offering courses, lessons, products, services, support, ideas, and dreams on how to be successful, happy, beautiful, rich — with a mere click of a button. If only we buy this guru's product containing this or that unprecedented wisdom — we will fulfill our dreams and finally be happy.

These deeply ingrained ideas dwell in people's hearts for years and keep them from realizing and utilizing their inner strengths. The spring of their unique nature, yearning to flow freely, is repressed. If a person feels inauthentic and in despair, how could they possibly inspire others?

People cannot live a fully satisfying life if they're busy mimicking others. It's a life as unstable as a house of cards, threatened to collapse with the slightest breeze. If we adopt other peoples' aspirations as our own instead of spreading our wings and venturing off, we will never reach our patch of heaven on Earth.

To develop the craft of persuasion — we must act out of a place of inner strength, tapping into the resilience and resources existing in every one of us. To do so, we must take off our masks and expose our true faces.

The time has come for us to shed the unnecessary layers of conditioning which had been wired into our brains. We must cast away our previous modes of thinking and peel away the veneer of inauthenticity with which society has covered us, particularly by those in power.

Don't forget — beneath those dusty layers lies the truth, your divine nature, yearning to be ignited once more. Beneath the rubble there is a fizzling spark waiting to burst into flames. Your flame.

Exposing your true self is the most important part of this long, eye-opening journey to paradise. Don't be mistaken, it'll take more than a three-day course or an inspirational book to get you there. Our journey begins with courage, a brave heart that is willing to open the doors to a room locked within us. To find the key, we must grant ourselves the right to be who we are. No more giving others the right to control us.

Once we internalize the motivation it will forge a surge of creativity and a natural knack to inspire and influence others. When you speak from a place of authenticity — and you no longer need others' approval — it clears the path leading to your goals.

Acting from a place of true, inner wisdom, we discover

fascinating things about ourselves. We might discover that our actual dreams and aspirations are vastly different from what others tried to force on us our whole lives. At this stage, we'll discover an immeasurable burst of energy oriented towards our actual goals. The moment we reach that summit, people around us will take notice of our effortless strength and will naturally gravitate toward us.

Exposing our uniqueness and ridding ourselves from the phoniness we have accumulated is a lifelong process — a personal journey spanning a lifetime of continuous learning and growing.

Nowadays, whenever I encounter a new situation, I discover something about myself I hadn't known before, some new trait that was hidden from my immediate experience. The first step on the way to creating our paradise begins with the courage to give ourselves permission to be unique. Let us no longer be confined to tiny cages created by others.

There's a story I like to tell when inspiring others to make a change. It's a story of two camels — a baby camel, the calve, and its mother.

One day, the baby camel asked its mother: "Mommy, why do we have a big hump on our backs?"

His mother replied with no hesitation: "Good question, son. We use it to store fatty tissue to help us survive days in the desert without water or food. We're an amazing animal, son."

The baby camel continued: "And Mommy, why do we have such long, thin legs?"

Once again the Mother had the perfect answer:

"Great question. We have long, thin legs to help us venture across sand for hours without getting tired. There's a reason they call us the 'ships of the desert.' We're an amazing animal, son."

The baby camel went on: "I have one final question, Mommy. Why do we have such long, thick eyelashes?"

His mother answered with joy: "Wonderful question. We have long, thick eyelashes to help us survive the ferocious sandstorms that plague the desert. We're an amazing animal, my sweet boy, never forget that."

Confused, little the baby camel lifted its gaze to its mom and pondered: "Then, why, Mommy, are we in the zoo and not out in the desert?"

In the blink of an eye, the years have passed and we've found ourselves locked in our own private cage, our own zoo. Is it comfortable? Of course! But is it keeping us back from venturing off to our real home? Yes. Superficiality and banality have become the hallmarks of our society, preferring to praise shallow illusions rather than profound truths.

Another tale tells of two cowboys. After a long day on the ranch, the two fellows sat by their horses on a hillside. One man was young, the other old. Suddenly, a gaudy cowboy gallops passed them on his horse, flashing a silver-plated saddle adorned with rare gems. The young cowboy, clearly impressed by the fancy horse, told his old partner: "Look at this impressive, noble horse. It'll surely take tomorrow's race."

The old cowboy, who had come across many horses in his time, chuckled and replied: "Son, after years of working with horses, I can confidently tell you that what we saw now was an expensive saddle, worth tens of thousands of dollars, on a cheap horse worth no more than 100 bucks. That horse won't win the race."

An impressive, expensive saddle won't turn any old horse into a winning one. In the same way, a fancy suit, a branded watch, or a coveted car won't turn a superficial person into a genuine leader.

When I look at my life, I view it as an archeological site. Now and then I venture on an excavation, digging deeper into my soul. I clean out the clutter to uncover new hidden gems and treasures I never knew existed.

The Robes of Power

At the start of my career as a lawyer, I longed to understand where traits like charm, charisma, and power came from. Why was it that only a small group of lawyers possessed those magical characteristics, enabling them to win so many cases? They were granted far more respect in the courtroom, from the judge, mere spectators, and even from their adversaries. On the other end of the spectrum were lawyers who were barely given a second glance and, if they happened to win a case, it was deemed a rare occasion that happened by pure chance.

I believe each one of us can recall meeting an important figure — a politician, religious leader, celebrity, etc. — and noticing a special aura about them, an energy that instantly drew us in. Perhaps we struggled to articulate a full sentence when in their presence.

The question arises — how can we develop that same aura and garner that same level of respect and admiration? How can we sound more convincing? Is the answer more money and more connections? Definitely not.

In fact, I believe that the only reason people have authority and power in the first place is because others have granted it to them.

Just as a king can't rule without his followers for, without their obedience, he is nothing but a normal person, so do we give power to the state. We're the reason our leaders have made it to the top.

At the start of my career I was scared to death when it came to facing big-shot lawyers from large firms, dressed like true aristocrats in lavish suits. To me, these lawyers were out of my league. At the time, I believed that the only way to outsmart them would be to use all measures to prevent them from stating their arguments. I would cut into their words, shrivel my face in disdain and call them out. I'd warn the judge not to fall for their 'goody two-shoes' act. Needless to say, that didn't take me far in life. I lost most of those cases and came out feeling like a failure.

At the end of a rowdy hearing I was the only one left in the courtroom, along with the judge. On our way out, the judge commented: "Lawyer Sofer, I suggest you take my advice and stop wasting all of your energy badmouthing the other lawyer." I stayed behind for a few moments contemplating his words when I realized my problem. By attacking the other lawyer I was, in fact, strengthening his status. I alone was to blame for my defeat. All of my attacks had made the opposing lawyer seem far more credible in the eyes of the judge.

A few years ago I was on vacation with my wife in

the north of Israel. On one of our hikes we came across a 50-year-old man who was walking at a similar pace. We ended up covering a host of interesting topics and discovered that the two of us shared a genuine love for nature and philosophy. After the day-long hike, we parted ways.

A few months later I met a good friend of mine, a fellow lawyer, at court. Having finished my hearing, I was free to enjoy a cup of coffee with him at the cafeteria. My friend, who still hadn't finished his day, went on about the complicated case he was working on and the stern judge who was handling it like a military officer. He offered me to join in and see for myself. Seeing as I thoroughly enjoy watching other lawyers in action, I agreed to come along.

Stepping into the courtroom with him I could tell how nervous he was, mainly because of the intimidating, hard-nosed judge. My friend took a seat at the defendant's table while I sat in the front row of benches intended for the public.

As both parties waited for the judge to arrive, the air grew so tense you could cut through it with a knife. My friend shifted around his chair, fidgeting with his tie as if it was a noose around his neck.

A few moments later, everyone leapt to their feet as the judge entered the courtroom and made his way to his seat. He ordered everyone to sit and flipped through the file before him.

I glanced at the judge, who looked terribly familiar. It took me a while to realize that he was the same man with whom I crossed paths on that hike up north. He recognized me too because, when our eyes met, he flashed a warm smile. The hearing paused for a moment as we greeted each other and exchanged a few polite words.

All the while my friend glanced at me in disbelief, stunned by how casually I was talking to this figure who, to him, was a complete threat.

In the course of the hearing, I pictured how I'd act if I was the one appearing before this judge. Chances are I would have represented my client with far more confidence than my friend.

Back when I crossed paths with him on the trail, he was just another hiker and nature-lover rather than a militant judge. I spoke freely, sharing my thoughts on cultural debates and philosophy without holding back or feeling self-conscious. My friend, however, treated this judge with such reverence that he was too scared to stand before him with confidence.

The authority and power of judges, as well as other impactful people for that matter, is strong simply because we allot them our veneration. If that's the case, why not keep this power for ourselves instead of blindly handing it to others?

To reach our paradise, we need to strengthen the reassuring voice within us: "You're doing great just as you are," and set aside taunting voices that hold too much acclaim for others, in a matter that is disproportionate and, eventually, at the expense of our own self-respect. Far too many people are prone to recoil and withdraw when encountering confrontations.

Permit yourselves to be who you are, to grant yourself that same level of respect and admiration. Once you do so, you'll see reality shift in your favor. Your posture will improve, your tone of voice will echo dominantly in the room, and word will spread about your charisma and appeal.

That being said, empowering ourselves is a slippery slope, as too much power can lead to corruption. The proper, dignified way to use that strength is to embrace it with humility, viewing it as a token granted to us to do good in the world. People in power must be accountable for their actions. Each and every one of us must take responsibility for our strength, always approaching it with caution.

Fear — A Shortcut to Heaven and Hell

Every human has an innate mechanism which, if used correctly, can empower them. This mechanism, however, doesn't come without a warning: if misused, it has the power to cripple us. Therefore, if this frightens you, skip to the next chapter.

I'm talking about the mechanism of fear. Not existential fear, or the survival instinct that gets our adrenaline pumping to flee from a lion; rather, the common psychological fear all of us experience, like stage fright, fear of standing out, fear of success, fear of starting a business, writing a book, getting married, or taking any substantial step in life.

This type of fear arises because we can't bear the thought of failure, of being disappointed, criticized and, in short, kicked out of our comfort zone. These aren't fears that put our very existence at risk, but rather prevent us from living the life we want.

How do we harness these fears and turn them into our motivating drive?

We'll start by reevaluating how we approach fear. Instead of viewing it as our enemy, we need to understand that it can be our ally, and a valuable one at that. While we know fear can shatter us, leading to a life of resentment and bitterness, we also know that the power it has over us depends on how we choose to deal with it when it arises.

As our enemy, fear can paralyze us, compelling us to avoid every possible challenge coming our way. If we take that path, we will find ourselves leaving a meaningless yet more 'comfortable' life. As our ally, however, fear can peak our alertness and help us prepare in advance for impending hardships.

When fear rises, our first instinct is to either freeze or flee. This is how most people in the world act, which explains why we seem so disoriented when stressed. But to befriend our fear we must first confront it, rather than repress and ignore. We must look it in the eye, letting it fill every cell of our body as it claws its way from our stomach to our chest. Yes, it may hurt, but along with the pain comes something else — an energizing, a feeling of vitality.

Imagine a deer living in the forest, peacefully drinking from the river, when suddenly it hears the snap of a branch breaking. Instinctively, it will stop what it's doing, lift its head, and perk up its ears. The surge of adrenaline running through its veins will stir the animal awake, readying it to escape potential danger. Rustling through the bushes, a hunter aims their gun at the animal. If the deer ignores the danger signals — it'll find itself on the hunter's plate.

In much the same way, we want to use our fear as an warning sign that can lead us to the right decision; as fuel, as a boost of energy shooting us forward toward our goals.

When I'm asked to speak in front of an audience, I often get nervous. I feel a sharp pang in my ribs, my stomach and feet grow heavy and my blood runs cold. Still, I've learned to acknowledge the fear and, even though it may hurt, I breathe into it. I take a deep breath, bravely glimpse at the audience and, for a few moments, engage in an inner dialogue between me and myself. It goes something like this:

Me 1: I'm scared. There are important people in the audience. I'll probably mess this up and embarrass myself. This talk isn't worth it if I end up becoming the laughingstock of the night.

Me 2: Yes, I'm scared. It's uncomfortable to leave my comfort zone and speak in front of a crowd. But there's no running away now. People have come to hear what I have to say. In fact, this is an opportunity to influence others by speaking about a topic I care about, a chance for me to get what I want. I'm doing it!

Me 1: Wait a minute. This isn't worth it. Don't you remember how you made a fool of yourself when you delivered that embarrassing toast at your grandfather's birthday a few years ago? Your family jokes about it to this day. It's better you tell everyone that you haven't prepared anything special. No one expects much from you anyway.

Me 2: True, I've messed up in the past. But I know how to speak to audiences. And I genuinely want to talk to them about this topic. That's it, I've made up my mind. I'm overcoming this fear and jumping head-first into the water. I'm doing it. I'm looking fear in the eye. One... two... three... go!

After this inner dialogue, I relax into my situation.

At times, when speaking in front of people, I picture myself at a pool, standing on a ten-meter-high springboard, about to jump into the water. On one hand, the thought of the jump brings about an exciting adrenaline rush but, on the other, I start trembling in fear, pondering over the few seconds I will be hanging in midair. Will I get a heart attack, or break my leg?

I take a few deep breaths and scrutinize the springboard. By fully embracing my fear, I'm filled with a vitality like never before. Finally, I count to three — and jump.

After the leap, I usually discover it wasn't that scary, that it was all part of my imagination. Time to relish in the celebratory cheers of the crowd!

Embrace your fear. Treat it as a wise instinct that can sharpen your senses. Use that raw energy to come up with the cleverest arguments and the best posture to engage and move those around you.

During one of my court appearances, when it was my turn to speak, I felt fear creep up and take control. I was scared that, if I blew this, my client would lose, costing him a sum of money he didn't have. I wanted to tame the fear but, instead, it took over and I froze.

"Yes, Attorney Sofer, what do you have to say in your client's defense in light of the prosecutor's accusations?" the judge called out. Blinking twice, I stared blankly into the distance until finally admitting: "I'm a bit nervous, your honor." The judge, who hadn't seen my confession coming, looked at me in amazement. Surely, he'd never expected an experienced lawyer to admit such 'weakness.' "I'm nervous I won't be able to present my case suitably, despite having prepared for this hearing for so long."

Miraculously, after admitting my fears to the judge, they went away. By putting my fear out there in the open, unknotting the bundle it created in my stomach, I gained the confidence I needed to present my arguments with far more impact.

In truth, I didn't care much about what the judge thought about me, and I surely wasn't looking for empathy or mercy. I admitted my fears to the judge so I could free myself from the burden and help my client win.

Whenever a fear arises, instead of fleeing or freezing, we'll make the conscious decision to charge forward and dive head-first into the water. After the initial jump, we'll see that the fear will dissipate and we'll be able to loosen up and present ourselves as we know we can.

Nowadays, I'm not ashamed to admit my fears. I'm not scared to say, "Look at me; I'm afraid." At first, I was wary about writing this book because I didn't know whether I'd have it in me to finish it. I was scared people wouldn't like the statements I made or the lessons I had to share. I was afraid to let others read it for fear they'd mock me or roll their eyes. I know, after all, that fear is a catalyst for growth. It's the fuel we need to advance and fulfill our dreams.

A brave person isn't someone who doesn't experience fear; it would be ignorant to think so. A brave person is someone who is afraid but nonetheless willing to overcome their fears to get what they want. In Judaism, there's a saying: *"A true hero is one who vanquishes their desires."* Your desire to flee, dear reader, should not dictate your life.

PART 2

Them

Heavenly Ties

Those close to us have nursed us from the moment we exited our mother's womb, and our loved ones will, hopefully, be there to bury us. Whichever way we look at it, the people around us play a hefty role in molding our lives. All of our dreams, aspirations, and goals are intertwined with the volition and energy of those in our surroundings. Whether it be the flourishing of our business, the upbringing of our children, or finding a life partner, we are forever entangled with and, in many cases, dependent on others.

For that reason, if our audience is wary of us, we will never be able to persuade them, despite the brilliant assertions we make. Only genuine connection can lead to true impact.

If your target audience fears you, no matter the reason, they will instantly block out your words, casting off even the wittiest of claims. Whatever attempt at convincing them will lead to more doubt, cynicism, aversion, misunderstanding, prejudice and, ultimately, complete disregard.

Upon hearing our pitch, our audience may squint their eyes, raise their brows, and express a general suspicion.

Their wariness may have nothing to do with us, but with their own, personal experiences. They may be hesitant about what they believe we represent. Or they may fear to come off as weak, spineless, and easily led by others. They may want to protect their sense of autonomy, their free will. Perhaps they worry about being disappointed or misled. There is no shortage of reasons when it comes to people's doubtfulness regarding others.

If we fail to mitigate this fear, we will face nothing but stubborn objections. Whatever claims we cook up will lead to evermore reluctance. So, before our audience rejects us, we must deal with the initial fear. This highlights a very important factor — if we manage to convince someone, it is only because they have granted us permission to do so.

When my eldest son was four, I took him to an speech therapist to help him pronounce certain letters properly. Walking into her room for the first time, we were greeted with mounds of toys and games. The therapist spent most of the session playing with and getting to know her little client. At first, this seemed to me a waste of time. Only later did I realize she had to win him over to get his cooperation. By the end of the meeting she had gained his trust and, thereby, was already able to work with him to improve his speech by the second meeting.

Conversely, a few months beforehand, my son suffered an eye infection after playing in the sandbox. I couldn't find a pediatric specialist at the time so I settled for an eye doctor who catered to adults instead. I thought they were the same, but unfortunately, I couldn't have been more wrong. The doctor had no patience and treated my son like just another item gliding along his factory's assembly line. Without any head up, the doctor examined my son's eye by stretching his hand out to his face. Understandably, my son recoiled in fear and tucked himself deeper into my arms. When the doctor tried lifting his head back to instill eye drops, my son bawled uncontrollably. He was so frightened that he refused any treatment from the scary man in white. No matter how hard I tried, I couldn't get him to cooperate. The kid was fixed in his ways and there was little we could do about it. The following day I took him to a pediatric ophthalmologist who was far more attuned to my son's needs. Her smile was warm and welcoming and her words were genuine and kind. After letting him roam the room and explore the different games, she attempted to instill the eyedrops. This time, of course, he agreed.

To influence others, we must first gain their trust. We do so by providing enough space for them to maneuver around our argument and decide for themselves whether they accept it. Much like eyedrops, it is impossible to forcefully instill in the eyes of the other our point of view.

Picture a large castle surrounded by a tall barricade, with guards ready to pounce on any intruder. The castle is impenetrable, encircled by a moat of hungry alligators. Unless the owner agrees to lower the bridge at the gate, there is no way to cross the perilous waters.

Each person is surrounded by a moat swarming with fear and reluctance. Fear of the person prying their eye open to instill drops, or fear of the person trying to convince them to buy a product, the logic is the same.

Once we dissolve those fears in others, we will get

them to open their gates and lower their bridge, granting us access to their kingdom.

Watch Your Speech

Semantics play a huge role in persuasion. The wrong word, either too intimidating or aggressive, can shut the client down. Accordingly, it's important to become aware of how we phrase our intentions and avoid any unnecessary impediments that will draw us further away from our goals.

From my experience as a lawyer, I've noticed a specific word that causes many to shrink away — for instance, 'contract.' Whenever I reach the concluding line of my pitch: "All that's left to do is to sign the contract..." the word 'contract' sends a pang of unease through their gut, and they are inclined to find a way to wriggle out of it.

Interestingly, if I exchange the word 'contract' with 'paper' or 'agreement': "to move forward I suggest we sign the papers" or "the agreement is ready, I just need your approval," there's a higher chance that the client will be willing to proceed. It's important to note the use of the words 'just' or 'I suggest,' which drastically reduces the enormity of signing a paper. Moreover, the word 'approval' comes off as less overwhelming than the dramatic commitment of 'signing' something.

'To sign' signals an act of no return which, naturally, scares off the clients who feel they're not willing to make this interminable bond. For example, if a business owner tells their client "Please sign this service-fee contract so I can begin my work," the response may often be a slight muttering of the words: "I need to think about it" or "It's a bit pricey."

Our choice of words has the power to bring up uncomfortable memories. Indeed, the fear people have of certain words is a conditioning of past experiences, like signing a contract they deeply regret, or recalling the reaction of their partner who glared at them in disappointment, yelling: "You idiot! They've fooled you, again! Don't sign anything without my permission!" These memories, stashed deep in their minds, spring forward whenever the act of signing is presented.

Another example: Instead of saying: "our product is worth $4,000" or "Our service fee is $4,000," it would be better use the word 'investment' instead — "there is only a $4,000 investment on your part." Investing in something comes off as lucrative, for it signals a future return on our expenditure.

Instead of the word 'purchase,' which may awaken some guilt-ridden demons of the past, taunting them for previously purchasing something entirely unnecessary, we'll use the phrase 'ownership of...' People love 'owning' assets. If salespeople are trying to get their client to purchase a car worth $50,000, they should say something along the lines of: "By investing only $50,000, you will become the proud owner of this magnificent car. Please approve this paper so we can move forward."

Some words work like magic, while others scare people off. We won't always know which ones to choose but we should, at the very least, become aware of how we frame our arguments. All things considered, aim for words that reduce your audience's fear and boost their sense of trust.

Our Innate Fear of the Other

Fear overflows from humans like foam spilling out of a glass full of beer. These deeply rooted fears highlight our innate nature as fragile, insecure beings.

We fear others, in part because we are afraid of getting carried away or losing ourselves. When it comes to persuasion, fear will intrude every time we ask someone to do something for us. If we don't detonate this ticking bomb with caution, it will explode in our face and cost us our deal.

Resisting persuasion is understandable, as it requires a certain level of self-control and authority. After all, when you want to coerce someone to agree with you, you're basically trying to gain control over their will and steer it in your direction.

Surely, your client will feel slightly robbed of their own autonomy. If pushed it to the edge, they might do things they've never dreamt of, resulting in a sense of betrayal. Much like poison spreading rapidly through our bodies, fear courses through our minds uncontrollably, shutting us out from offers, both sketchy and legit.

People will often say "no" as a means of gaining a renewed sense of control over their fragile ego. To tap into people's reasoning process, we should strengthen their sense of dominance in the conversation. We should create a space for our audience to feel secure and in control. The moment they feel free to calmly consider their decision, without making any commitment, they'll be far more open to hearing what we have to say. The best way to do so is by granting our audience full permission to say no. By doing so, their initial resistance will magically vanish.

While it's true that opening the possibility of rejection may eventually lead to rejection, we need to keep in mind that the alternative of wariness and suspicion is far worse. If our audience is intimidated by us — no amount of clever words will convince them otherwise. We should renounce means of aggression and force for a gentle approach instead. Even if we don't reach our desired result, ending on good terms has long-lasting repercussions. Who knows, they might slip in a good word about us to their neighbor.

When clients first arrive at my office for legal representation, I often notice how wary they are of accepting my service. Stepping into the room, they sit with their hands crossed, unsure of whether I'm the right lawyer for them. Some will even reject my friendly offer of coffee. Before I get any words across, I need to help them regain their sense of power over the situation. Therefore, one of the first things I say is: "This meeting is, first and foremost, for consultation purposes. I'm going to give you my take on your legal situation. Even if you end up going with a different lawyer, I can, at least, offer you a second opinion. As a rule, I advise visiting several lawyers to ensure you're confident enough when making your choice."

My easygoing, unhurried words are precisely what my clients need to loosen up. They come to realize that

I'm not trying to force them into anything. At first, they nearly always approach the matter with natural suspicion, possessively clinging to their free will. Surely, it'll take more than a bit of charisma to get them on board. What they need is a sense of control. Once they reclaim it, my clients will have their ears open to my suggestions and consider my services with far more earnest.

Desperate to control the conversation, people often make the mistake of using words like 'must' or 'have to' in the hopes of forcing their opinions onto others. Of course, no one likes to be shoved into doing something, especially if we never wanted to in the first place. We like feeling as if our choices stem from a place of free will, from the depths of our own, personal volition. For that reason, words with an air of impatience and urgency might scare us off.

If a salesman approaches me and stresses that I absolutely 'have to' buy their product, I automatically shut down and assert that I don't 'have to' do anything. I 'have to' breathe air or drink water to survive, but I certainly don't 'have to' buy the product they're selling.

Of course, we can find ourselves using these enthusiastic words when talking with a friend or recommending a new item we've recently tried, but in that case, we're being friendly, not aggressive. For example, when a friend recommends a new restaurant in town: "You simply have to go to the new Italian place near your house."

When persuading others, it's best to use soft words, ones that sound modest and contemplative. I often begin my pitch with: "You don't have to..." — a simple opening line that automatically relaxes everyone in the room.

"Look, David, you don't have to hire our services. There are plenty of young lawyers willing to represent you for half the price in order to gain experience." Once I've laid that out, the client instantly perks up their ears.

Unsurprisingly, the words 'have to' or 'must' are often used by couples who are entangled in an obsessive relationship. This word might help us get the job done but, in reality, it's like oil fueling an already raging fire, sparking a flurry of volatile arguments.

Instead of shriveling our faces in anger, yelling: "You have to take down the trash today;" "You must relax;" "You have to pick the kids up today," it's better to say: "I'd love for us to spend the holidays at my parents" or "How about we go on vacation next week?"

One phrase is constructive; the other is destructive.

Another way to loosen up our audience is by adding reassurances such as: "I'm not forcing you into anything" or "It's your decision."

Thus, for example, a lawyer can tell their client: "David, I've explained everything there is to know about how we can steer this case in your favor. But, honestly, no one can force you into anything. It's a decision you will have to make."

In this case, the lawyer has given their client full permission to turn them down, strengthening the idea that the ball is in their court.

The word 'maybe' is often overlooked and, while it may appear innocent, it radiates an unhurried position in which we're giving our clients enough leeway to think for themselves.

"What do you say, maybe we'll visit my parents this

weekend?" Behind this innocent suggestion is a burning desire to pay one's family a visit. However, being as it was proposed so innocently, the other partner will surely feel the need to consider it.

Even words like 'can you...' when proposed as a question, soften our audience and raise the chances of fulfillment.

For example: "Can you please pour me a glass of water?" instead of a demanding statement such as, "Pour me some water." In short, 'can you...' is a polite call for action.

The Magic of Modesty

Another way to get people on board is by expressing humility. By this, I mean seemingly 'undervaluing' yourself in order to let the other shine. As a rule, no one likes a know-it-all, and people generally are turned off by traits such as arrogance and pride. We enjoy being around down-to-earth people who respect our opinions and give us a sense of worth. With that in mind, I purposely 'undervalue' myself before my clients to make them feel in charge of the situation.

For instance, let's say a lawyer appears in court and wants to convince the judge that Section 8 of the Contract Law falls in line with the arguments he made in the statement of claim. The lawyer can apply this technique and argue before the judge as follows:

"Your Honor, I'd like to present you with my assessment of Section 8 of the Contract Law. Surely, your honorable judge can teach me a thing or two about interpreting the ruling regarding this section, and I am deeply grateful for the opportunity to explain why my client's claims must be accepted. I assure you, your honor, that they are in line with extensive past ruling as well as scholarly opinions."

Right off the bat, the lawyer has admitted that the judge has much to teach them about Section 8. This humility will soften the judge, who, after hearing such words, will be far more disposed to listen.

Let us not confuse 'devaluation' with 'humiliation.' We are certainly not interested in making a joke of ourselves or belittling our competence before the crowd. Acting from a place of modesty is done cleverly, calmly, and with the end goal always in mind.

Mastering Body Language

Our bodies will always reveal our emotions no matter how hard we try to hide them. When we're sad, our tone of voice may tremble and soften, almost to a whisper. When we're happy, our lips will curl into a smile, making it nearly impossible to keep our inner worlds a secret.

There's a strong reciprocal link between our emotions and body language. Tightly intertwined, our bodies reflect our emotions, and our emotions can be altered by shifting our bodies. If our boss humiliates us at work, for example, we will instantly shrivel and withdraw into our chair. If, upon returning home, we bounce on the trampoline in our backyard with hands in the air, screaming: "Yay, yay, yay!" we'll almost surely loosen up.

Even though our tone of voice can also disclose our

emotions, it's easier to manipulate. In contrast, our bodies shift so subtly that we barely notice. If your boss yells at you, your response may be calm, using just the right words to mask your inner turmoil. However, remembering to straighten your slouched back or loosen your clenched fists will be harder. These small shifts in movement seem to fleet our awareness.

Unbeknownst to us, whenever we interact with people, our brains are busy detecting whether their body language matches the words coming out of their mouths. The more congruency, the more credibility they gain, and vice versa. If someone expresses how delighted they are to see us, yet mutters the words with an air of indifference — clearly, they're not very happy.

If our body language expresses suspicious signs like peering nervously around the room to avoid eye contact, the person before us will automatically begin to wonder what's wrong. As soon as this red flag appears, our audience will become cautious and defensive, making it harder for us to get through to them.

After witnessing countless people express themselves in court, particularly lawyers, I've come to realize that our bodies are a valuable tool. As long as we're oblivious to how we move, we're at the risk of tarnishing our credibility, ultimately ruining our chance to make an impact. Crossed arms, clenched fists, hands deep in pockets or resting impatiently on our hips — come off as anti-social and negative.

We should become aware of the subtleties of our bodies and rid ourselves of the fidgety movements that seem, at best, weak and, at worst, suspicious. We need to move our bodies with precision, in a way that is attuned to our speech.

Credibility — Our One-Way Ticket to Paradise

There are many ways we can influence people and each method has its pros and cons. Depending on our target audience, we will adjust our strategy accordingly. Despite the differing tactics, however, there's one indispensable foundation, a trait every person should adopt if they want to influence others. Without it, we can toss our clever strategies aside.

I'm talking about credibility. This may seem obvious, but many people ditch this essential component and thus sabotage their chances of affecting others. Our credibility can compensate for whatever flaws we have, such as lack of experience if you seem unreliable, whatever wonderful sales tactics you prepared will come tumbling down like a house of cards.

For me, the courtroom serves as the perfect lab to test which tools and strategies work. I've witnessed talented lawyers deliver impeccable performances only to lose due to their shaky credibility. If the judge doesn't believe a word you say, your polished speech will fall on deaf ears.

I once managed a case along with a lawyer who was considered the best and brightest in his field. He had sharp wits and a brain that could rapidly process the crossfire of words in the courtroom. Whatever came out of his mouth was ingenious, quick-witted, and brilliant. That being said, he lost quite a lot of cases, which came as a surprise for many. The simple reason was his lack of credibility. He was slightly devious and had a habit of stretching the truth in his client's favor. Every time a judge called him out, he would whip out a clever excuse to wipe his reputation clean. Despite managing to sweet talk his way out of some sticky situations, his overall untrustworthy nature was palpable. Gradually, his clients ditched him.

When we're trustworthy, our audience will be willing to listen, granting us a prize opportunity to influence their opinions. When we adhere to the truth, our body language, as well as our tone of voice and choice of words, synchronizes harmoniously like an orchestra following a conductor's swift fingers. When we act deviously, tiptoeing our way around things, a scratch of the nose, a slight cough, a sudden hoarseness of the voice, a stuttering, a flickering of the eyes, etc. — our bodies will give us away. Incredibility causes those around us to be wary, suspicious and, eventually, unwilling to listen.

Being credible means being authentic, transparent and honest. No one likes a phony, just as no one appreciates a fake diamond necklace. We appreciate authenticity and admire shows of vulnerability and candidness. Our trustworthiness allows those around us to relax and open their minds to what we have to say.

Anyone can gain credibility, but this requires a level of devotion and a commitment to being open about our thoughts and emotions. Even though it doesn't always cater to our interests, truth holds great power and there's no denying the strength it has over people.

The art of persuasion calls for peoples' most precious

asset: their trust. If you were lucky enough to earn it, this indicates that your audience was willing to be vulnerable, at your disposal. For this to happen, you must be prepared to be vulnerable yourself, willing to expose your flaws and weak spots.

If you're feeling nervous, don't hide behind a forced smile. Admit it. You'll be surprised by people's reactions. On the flip side, your client will feel deceived if they feel you're hiding something.

We're wired to steer clear from untrustworthy people who may endanger us and, instead, seek the company of credible, honest people who we can read fairly easily. We prefer transparency over uncertainty, even if we don't always agree with what is being brought to the table.

That being said, we shouldn't overdo our emotions or wear them on our sleeves for the whole world to see. Moderation is key. If you sound too pitiful or miserable, people will find it hard to empathize with your story. Your motives may even become suspect.

Sadly, some lawyers don't mind scheming and manipulating to win a trial. They do so willingly, using sly tricks to steer the case in their direction. Luckily, an attentive judge will catch on to their bluff and rule against most of their preposterous claims.

Plainly stated, we cannot expect to gain people's trust if we're not willing to open up ourselves. It doesn't matter if we're trying to sell something, win a trial, or convince our partner to listen — trustworthiness is our ticket to success.

Here's a story that brilliantly captures this matter:

There once was an explorer who ventured far and wide to one of the densest jungles in the world. He and his crew were seeking a remote tribe living far from the throes of civilization. At one point, the explorer lost track of his crew. Luckily, he was armed, relying on his knives and rifle to keep him safe, with enough food and water to last him a few days.

A week had passed, and still there was no sight of his crew. Living on a few scraps of food, he decided to walk to the nearest tribe and ask for help. But this wouldn't be an easy task, as the locals were known for their hostile suspicion and violent behavior, particularly toward armed outsiders. There was no point in trying to fight them as the numbers were, obviously, against him. So, after careful deliberation, he decided to gain their trust instead.

With hands in the air, he paced slowly into the village and rested his knives and gun at the chief's feet. "Water, food..." he pleaded. By exposing himself in front of these strangers, the explorer was taking a huge risk. But it was a wise decision. The locals, puzzled by this intruder's vulnerability, quickly understood that he meant no harm. They showered him with food and water and showed him the way out of the lush entanglement.

The locals could've easily taken advantage of the explorer's submission. Still, this was a risk worth taking. Without their trust, the man would've ended his life running circles in the bush, starved and dehydrated.

If we use conniving lies to get our way, we'll be sealing our fate as deceitful adversaries who cannot be trusted. Naturally, this will spark nothing but antagonism from people. However, if we lower our guns and put down our shields, our surroundings will do the same.

Our credibility is our strongest weapon. We must refrain from telling lies, as well as be honest about how we feel.

Burdened by a sense of shame and worry, it's natural to shy away from exposing our true thoughts and feelings. A client of mine once told me of a fight he had with his 18-year-old son at the dinner table. Young and eager, his child wanted to buy a heavy motorcycle, nearly causing my client a heart attack. He spent the next few days fuming over his son's reckless decision and announced that he wouldn't fund the driving lessons nor the bike.

Understandably, his son reacted with the same level of fury and quickly countered by claiming that he was old enough to decide for himself. He would use his savings to pay for the lessons and work overtime on the weekends to buy a bike.

Over the next few months, father and son bickered endlessly until, finally, the deal was done, and the son came home one day with a big, heavy motorcycle. By this point, they were barely talking.

With a grim face, my client opened up about the crumbling relationship and how his son no longer came to him for advice.

If my client had handled the case differently, perhaps approaching his son with a softness and openness that allowed for conversation, things would've ended differently.

My client undoubtedly loved his child, which is precisely why he was so worried about his riding a motorcycle. Blinded by his anxieties, he failed to acknowledge his son who, like many kids his age, simply craved the thrill and exhilaration of cruising with friends.

Consider how things might have turned out if this had been handled differently. For example, if the father would have responded as such:

"Son, I want you to know that I trust and love you with all of my heart. You're 18 and old enough to decide for yourself. But, before you do anything, hear me out." Approaching the matter with humility and love, the father is ready to expose himself and his fears, opting for connection (predicated on vulnerability) as opposed to alienation (predicated on impulsive reactions like unnecessary yelling).

"I'm genuinely scared that something bad will happen to you; I'm terrified of the thought that you might get into an accident; I'm scared that I won't be able to help you; I'm scared of losing you."

Putting himself out there, the dad's words carry a powerful tone that no son can ignore. The father's candidness will strike his son as a commendable show of bravery, allowing for actual conversation in which both sides can be heard. Without this element of trust, there is no way to bridge the gap between both conflicting sides.

Unable to disregard his dad's honest outpouring of emotion, the son now has to decide how to react. He might calm his father by saying: "Dad, I care for how you feel, and the last thing I want is to hurt you. Trust me, I won't risk my life by driving around like a maniac.

But buying a motorcycle has been a dream of mine for years, and I'm not willing to give it up." In this case, even though the father has failed to change his son's mind, he has still managed to save their relationship. He knows that his son cares for him and that he will do his utmost to drive safely.

Another option is a change of heart: "Dad, I had no idea you felt this way. A lot of my friends are getting a motorcycle license, so I thought it would be cool to get one myself. On second thought, maybe I should go for a car instead... can you help me pay for some of the lessons?"

One of my friends, a family law solicitor, told me why his clients are happy to have him represent them in their divorce proceedings. When clients come to him for an initial consultation, he shares the story of his own difficult divorce. By being vulnerable, he's able to ignite feelings of empathy, establishing a good foundation from which to begin their work together.

By exposing our weaknesses, we're encouraging our surroundings to do the same. A good, solid rapport is formed, allowing our empathic words to tug on people's heartstrings.

Every minor cough or fidgeting of the hands; every slight change of tone, or brief twitch of the mouth; nervous blinking or heavy breathing; every bit of information our subconscious swiftly perceives in a fraction of a second— will mark whether the person before us is worthy of our trust. For better or worse, we've been gifted these 'credibility detectors' — a brilliant survival mechanism.

These detectors home in on lies and manipulations, shielding us from people who are out to fool us.

This isn't some mystical, sixth-sense granted only to the enlightened. This is an innate skill, passed on to us by our ancestors who once lived in caves and survived in the wild. Lying was considered a sin. Those who lied were disowned from the tribe, and for good reason. They posed a danger to the delicate fabric of the clan.

Our intuitions about the other are often justified , even if we cannot always confirm them. While we won't always have conclusive proof of our gut feelings, we should still pay close attention to them. The speed at which our subconscious processes the other's body language is amazingly faster than the time it takes our conscious mind to come up with the right words to explain the situation at hand.

In conversation, our brain processes an enormous amount of information, comparing it to previous experiences and memories. By doing so, it catches on to beneficial patterns that help us make sense of the world.

Persuasion, no matter how creative, is limited to the amount of trust someone puts in us.

For some reason, though, some people decide to present their arguments before winning their client's trust. Trust, however, should be our utmost priority; the first thing we seek when approaching people.

A skilled, articulate salesperson may know the tactics to reel a person in. They may know how to respond swiftly to any objection, combating rejections with an admirable air of confidence. But if he lacks credibility — his pitch will fail.

Politicians are a fantastic example. On the one hand, they come off as important figures who know how to carry themselves with grace. They are masters at speaking to the camera and whipping out fast, witty replies against interviewers' merciless attacks. But most politicians are tragically unreliable, and no level of eloquence can save them from the crowd's disdain and suspicion.

In much the same way, lawyer, no matter how quick-witted, will fail to win a trial if they lack credibility. This, of course, takes into account the court's integrity, as well as the time frame designated for the trial. Jurors can fall into their traps at first but, over time, their credibility detectors will eventually kick in and catch on.

Although we're good at shielding ourselves from our enemies, we often fail to avoid people who claim to be our friends but actually are not. When a person is openly malicious, we can arm ourselves accordingly. However, when caught off guard by someone who claims to have our best interests in mind, our response time will be delayed, and we are left defenseless and unprepared for the sudden battle.

Our chances of falling into the trap of a sly fraud are far higher than that of a person who is straight-out malicious. For that reason, we must keep our 'credibility detectors' polished and at the ready, as it is our only hope of navigating safely through the human jungle.

Credibility — An Important Lesson in Emotions

To come off as honest, we need to be candid about our feelings. Even though this leaves us vulnerable and exposed, it is the risk we need to take to master the art of persuasion, and the step needed to create the life we want for ourselves.

Emotions are highly personal, our intimate secret. For this reason, sharing our feelings more easily turns us into trustworthy partners.

The emotions we express make us reliable, as they stem from a genuine part of our inner being and are treated as credible sources precisely because they're hard to fake.

They're the window to our soul, allowing for a brief glimpse into our human experience. As soon as we open up to each other — the walls of doubt and cynicism crumble and our exchange of words becomes more gentle and honest.

Emotions enrich the fabric of our lives, adding a variety of shades and colors to our otherwise bland reality. As painters have a myriad of colors on their palettes, we, too, should have a myriad of emotions at our disposal. Even if we don't feel the full scope of every sensation, we should, at the very least, learn how to express it.

The 'colors' we use to express ourselves include anger, compassion, refusal, reparation, indifference, sadness, pain, fear, joy, happiness, boredom, disgust, awe, love, security, hope, justice, and more. These emotions 'color' our body language, syncing our behavior with our inner world.

Most people struggle to express such richness of emotion, which is why they fail to appear reliable and authentic.

Do you remember how, as a kid, you were able to

express whatever emotion came up? As adults, we often feel a pang of jealousy when we witness how kids behave, with their rolling laughter echoing freely in the air. Or when we see them burst into tears when they're feeling scared, furrow their brows when their dad isn't willing to buy them a gift, or scrunch their face in disgust when eating something they don't like. Emotions come naturally to kids, which is precisely why they're so convincing (and able to get what they want). In fact, the best teachers of authenticity are kids. They have something that we, unfortunately, have lost over the years.

When we were kids, we wanted to be grown-ups. The grown-up world seemed boundless and fun, without any restrictions, like when to eat or when to go to bed. Ironically, though, as adults, we try to become kids again. We crave that sense of naïve enthusiasm and curiosity over the wonders of life.

If you have the chance, spend some time with kids, but make sure that you're putting your heart into whatever game they propose. This may seem weird at first but don't hold back. Allow yourself to be a child, for just a few moments, and put down your guard. You'll soon develop spontaneous reactions, laughing for no reason or getting excited over a bed that has been transformed into an imaginary spaceship.

At one point in our lives, we began to hide our emotions, cloaking them under layers of cold rationale and a serious front. We've tossed our hearts aside in favor of cold, rigid, logic.

This shouldn't come as a surprise — our society,

after all, doesn't encourage displays of emotion. When compared to logical reasoning, speaking from the heart is deemed irrational and silly. From elementary school to university, we're judged for our intellect (even though most of our decisions are sparked by emotions).

Most people don't remember what it's like to burst into uncontrollable laughter or genuinely rejoice. Much like a clogged pipe filled with unnecessary junk, people's ability to let loose has been blocked by layers of clutter they've accumulated over the years. When people finally do end up laughing, many can only manage is a polite grin and a few chuckles, remnants of their childhood. Of course, such a flat response cannot ignite any emotion in others, nor can it move or influence people.

How can we open ourselves up to the world again, utilizing the gift of emotions to persuade and inspire?

Firstly, we can turn to music. The sweet melodies we once listened to can lift our spirits in an instance, tapping into the child within us. When the lyrics begin, sing. I recommend finding a place where you can be on your own. Go for a walk and find your spot. It can be a vacant shore, the woods, or even your backyard.

Alone with nature, breathe deeply, and let the touch of soil melt into your hands. If you come across a flower, stroke its petals and take in the smell.

Try to silence your thoughts. Be present with your surroundings. Immerse yourself in your natural habitat by noticing small changes, like the rustling of trees, the swaying of waves, or the flight of a nearby insect.

Now, how about a song?

Certainly, by this point, the rational voice in your

head may convince you otherwise. "Stop it... you look stupid..."

If this is too hard for you, feel free to jump to the next chapter (where practical strategies can be found). Sitting in silence takes time, and is quite intimidating at first.

If you have decided to stick around, let the voice in your head come as it is. Ignore its cynical tone, and keep going.

Time to sing.

You might keep your voice low and hesitant at first but, as you proceed, you'll gradually raise the tone, allowing the words to ring out into the open.

You might peer to the right, then to the left, worried that someone may be watching. After all, you don't want to come off as 'crazy.' But don't bother darting your eyes from one corner to the next. Instead, focus on yourself, your experience, your emotions. Stop worrying about what others may think. You are the center of your universe now, the sole actor of your play. For some, this may be the very first time they come across such intimacy.

Once you've briefly sang a tune, or hummed some words, decide on an emotion you want to express. Choose a word, any word, and belt it out with rage.

For example: "rrrrrrrrrrrrrrrrrrrrrrrrrrrrr"

At first, you might feel quite funny, unable to pour the actual emotion into the sound. It'll sound forced and inauthentic. Do it again.

"rrrrrrrrrrrrrraaaaaaarrrrrrrrr"

It's okay if you still feel self-conscious. It takes a while to rid ourselves of these intrusive thoughts.

Do it until you feel you've done it right. This is how you learn to tap into your genuine emotions.

Now, choose a word that reflects joy.

"Yaaaaaaaaaayyyyyyyyyy"

Repeat it, again and again, until you genuinely feel happy. Feel free to raise your hands in the air or jump.

The same technique goes for sadness, enthusiasm, anger, love, compassion, etc.

Observe the nature around you. How about some words of release? Words of gratitude for what it has taught you?

Choose a sentence, and express it with the full range of whichever emotion you choose:

"I'm full of ___ and I want to thank ___"

"I believe I am ___ and he isn't ___"

"What is happening to me, I am ___ and also ___"

"It is said that ___, which is why I am ___"

Expressing emotions through words helps us connect, not only with nature but with ourselves. By bonding with the world around you, you'll find that you're bonding with parts of yourself you have long forgotten.

In the past, humans were far more in tune with nature. We slept on the ground and walked barefoot across sand and soil. We grew our food and bathed in the river. The connection was immediate and direct. Today, however, we are detached from our natural surroundings, enclosed between concrete walls, our feet tucked into tidy shoes.

Before you finish this session, listen to the sounds around you. Depending on where you are, you may hear birds chirping, leaves rustling, or the trickling of a flowing river. Lingering in the background of this scene is a serene silence. Listening so attentively may feel weird at first, but it's a crucial turning point from which you can develop a child-like wonder again.

It isn't easy to loosen up, especially if you've conditioned yourself to the point of total rigidity. It takes courage to break free from the prison you've built within yourself. For some, it's a lifelong journey, nevertheless an invaluable one. Remember, our emotions set the tone of our words and serve as a crucial tool in persuasion.

Whenever genuine emotions accompany our arguments, we come off as trustworthy, regardless of whether the person agrees with what we have presented. Keep in mind, though, that exaggerated, over-the-top displays of feelings often appear sketchy. Don't overdo your emotions.

In my years as a lawyer, I've learned the value of standing face-to-face with the judge, keeping my gaze steady, and speaking candidly. Whether pain, frustration, fury, joy, or enthusiasm — a diverse range of emotions is laced into my arguments, creating a powerful act that cannot be ignored.

In contrast, when I submit a written request on behalf of my clients, I don't rely on emotions to get me far. I look for the most precise and accurate words to convey their needs. Compared to the rich, spirited performance of body language presented in person, printed words on a sheet of paper are slightly more polished and composed.

Written requests are formed in the comfort of my office, where I feel at home. In stark contrast, the courtroom doesn't provide the same comforting conditions.

In front of an audience, a surge of emotions course through my veins, pulsing with the rest of the energy in the room — the nerves of my client, the combativeness of the opposing attorney, and the scrutinizing eye of the judge. I find myself pacing back and forth, suit drenched in sweat, words drawn out of my mouth with raw honesty. The impact of my extensive presentation is far more influential than the tidiness of words in print.

Don't Sabotage Your Relationships — Control Your Emotions

Perfecting the art of persuasion will help us achieve the things we want, taking us one step closer to our ideal life. Of course, we won't always have the ideal conditions to express ourselves impeccably, and some factors will divert us from what we initially had in mind. These factors include our emotions. In the previous chapter, we spoke about the power emotions have to establish credibility and authenticity. In this chapter, we'll discuss the bumps we might encounter along the road if we don't learn how to control them.

I'm sure we can all recall a moment of anger that erupted from what started as an innocent interaction. Maybe we lost control and inadvertently slipped in an insult. This happens when we try to express the importance of a certain value or goal but, sadly, end up forcing the person to agree with our perspective. Our ego claws its way into the arena, and we begin to wrestle with the other person's opinion. Eventually, both sides remain unconvinced, restrained to their own worldview.

When our request is met with a cold, piercing "no" it echoes in our minds like the continuous ring of a burning slap on the cheek (especially coming from someone we care for). The obvious affront causes tensions to rise, bubbling, at times, to the point of screams and finger-pointing, each side accusing the other of lying, cheating, and overall malice.

When this happens, all of the tools and strategies presented in this book (or any other self-help manual) will amount to zero. Overflowing with rage, we won't be in the right mindset to apply any new skills, no matter how useful. Our chances of persuading the other will be gobbled by our unruly emotions.

Picture this

After a long day's work, a husband returns home and, without greeting his wife, plops onto the couch. Zipping through channels on the TV, his only desire is to zone out and relax. Suddenly, his wife appears, eyes brimming with enthusiasm. She reminds him of the promise he had made to take her to dinner that night to celebrate her new job. The husband feels frustrated that his wife doesn't realize how exhausted he is. Is she aware of how hard he's been working lately? And anyway, how did she even remember that silly promise he made a week ago? The husband politely asks his wife to postpone dinner to a later date. "I'm not feeling well," he explains. The wife isn't buying into his excuse. Instead, she focuses on his intolerable aloofness.

At first, the couple tries to behave in a civilized

manner, presenting their case in a relatively composed way. Unfortunately, whatever etiquette they flexed at the beginning is quickly tossed aside, as both sides withdraw deeper into their position. Next thing you know, the boxing gloves are whipped out, ready to punch the other into submission. Husband and wife toss painful memories into the air, full of blame and shame and insult. As the match advances, each side spirals into bitterness and frustration, knowing very well that the argument is leading nowhere.

How do we tame these emotions that wash over us in a fraction of a second, right under our noses? How do we make rage, resentment, frustration, and pain work in our favor?

Firstly, we need to understand that the process of persuasion never calls for forcing our opinions on others, nor should we poke people's consciences as a form of getting them to concede to us. Such behavior will tarnish our chances of achieving our goals. Our ego may get a temporary boost out of it, but that is certainly not the point.

In such cases, we're left with two options. The first is to 'give in' to those emotions, trudging blindly behind as they lead us to a dead-end. The result is a demolishing tornado that will swallow our relationships whole.

The second option is to control these emotions and channel them elsewhere, using their power to move things in the right way to maintain our relationships healthy and sane.

Back when I was a teenager, we had an 80-year-old next-door neighbor. Every Saturday morning, her son would drop by for a visit, and the two would spend their first half hour together arguing relentlessly. The cross-fire of words was so loud that the whole neighborhood was in on the show. It went something like this:

Mom: "Jonathan, why don't you spend your Saturdays at the synagogue like your brothers?"

Jonathan: "Mom, you know I haven't been to the synagogue in years. I'm not a kid anymore. I can do what I want."

Out of frustration, the mom replies: "You know the kind of hell that awaits sinners... is that where you want to find yourself?"

Naturally, the son loses his patience and yells: "Mom! Enough with that. I'm sick of hearing the same thing over and over again. You know I don't believe in that nonsense. I should've hung out with my friends instead of coming here."

Mom: "How about you find yourself a good wife and settle into family life, like your brothers? You're not getting any younger, you know. If you don't get your life together, you'll end up like your uncle — alone and childless." The mom uses her words as swords, piercing her son's frail heart.

By this point, her son lashes out: "Mom, this is my life, and I'll choose how to live it. Stop butting into everything. I'm not like my brothers. Ugh! I'm tired of coming here. It's always the same..."

Mom: "I know you don't care about me. If your brothers weren't here to look after me, I'm sure you would've tossed me to a nursing home years ago. The only thing you care for is your inheritance." Another stab in the heart.

In response to her bitter comments, the son replies cynically: "You know what? Now that you mention it... a nursing home doesn't sound that bad. You can find yourself new bingo friends. More importantly, you'll stop getting on my nerves. I know a really good place up north." Seeing his mom's nervous expression, the son feels proud of himself and even goes so far as to look up the place on his phone.

Startled, the mom responds: "Jonathan, don't you dare! I'll take you out of my will. I want to die in the comfort of my own home, not in some run-down nursing home, do you hear me?!"

Ignoring her, the son goes on: "Here, I found it. Ahh, the view looks amazing. It seems a bit old, but definitely affordable."

The mom yells: "Enough, Jonathan! You'll end up killing me."

After both sides are fed up with the hostile drama, they wrap up the play, both actors bleeding on stage. The conversation ends and each move on.

When we feel angry, whatever the reason, our go-to response is to unleash the beast and let it roam freely. But this untamed emotion will crush every chance we have of leading things in the direction we want.

If we choose to bottle up our emotions and repress this boiling energy, it'll end up devouring us from within. And if we hurl our feelings at the other person, we risk ruining our chances of reaching an agreement. In either case, we fail to influence and persuade others in our favor.

The proper solution is to let go of these emotions,

slowly and carefully, just as bombs are detonated in a controlled manner to avoid deadly explosions.

When we feel that our partner has offended us, it won't help to lash out at them, nor will it help to keep the hurt to ourselves. The best way out of it is by exposing our feelings with genuine calm and admitting the hurt with an open heart.

If I feel that someone is lying to me, I'll confess: "To be honest, I feel quite cheated by the offer you made." That way, I'm putting my emotions out there and creating a space for honest interaction. The wrong way to go about it would be to snap at the person before me: "Listen, you're one hell of a liar, and your offer is nothing more than a big disgrace." Surely, these words will do nothing but upset the other person.

When speaking to a friend of mine, I'll say: "I've felt offended by your words lately. Have I done something to hurt you?" Instead of: "You keep insulting me! Enough already!"

By controlling our emotions and releasing them with composure, we're able to shed light on our personal experience, as opposed to blaming the other. We aim to free ourselves of the uncomfortable, stored energy so we can feel better and less resentful.

One time during a court hearing, I began to feel as if the judge was being particularly hard on me, for no apparent reason. Every argument I posed or every request I put out on behalf of my client was met with a stubborn, dismissing wave of the hand. I felt frustrated and hurt, completely inept at representing my client.

After presenting one argument, the judge accused me

of repeating myself incessantly, I approached the judge's bench and admitted to feeling frustrated for failing to articulate myself appropriately in the trial. I then turned around and took my seat.

The judge didn't respond, nor did she apologize but, from that point on, she refrained from commenting on my words so often. I felt much more at ease and was able to present my claims with regained composure. If I had decided to keep my frustration to myself, I would have, at best, failed to present my arguments appropriately and, at worst, spiraled into an argument with the judge, neither of which would've helped my client win the case.

Anger is a secondary emotion as it is fueled by a prior sensation, like pain, fear, or insecurity. Therefore, instead of lashing out at our audience, we'd better take a step back and examine its roots.

Creating our heaven on Earth requires self-regulation, one of the toughest skills to acquire. Even if we think we've reached the point of complete equanimity, sooner or later, a new hurdle will come tumbling our way.

Better weather the storm with calm.

Stepping Into the Other's Shoes — Heaven's Best Viewpoint

The best way to understand someone is by putting ourselves in their position. By stepping into their shoes, we develop empathy and a sincere interest.

Once we relate with others, we can start to influence them on a deeper level.

Empathy is an amazing tool and is tragically overlooked by people who prefer to focus only their own point of view. Confined within the walls of their stubborn minds, they're blind to the other's needs.

To develop a deeper understanding of the another's situation, we will attempt to embody the life of the person in front of us. In this unique state of compassion and empathy, we will listen to the person before us and ask relevant, caring questions. With the use of attentive body language and a thoughtful tone of voice, we'll strengthen the bond with reassuring phrases: "I understand;" "This must be hard for you;" "I've felt that way too."

By putting ourselves in the other's shoes, we learn to speak their language. Not only will we succeed in understanding them better, but they, too, will feel an instant connection to us. Once this fruitful bond has sprouted, any claims or suggestions we bring up from now on will have far more impact.

I once represented a real estate agent at a court hearing. He was suing a young man who refused to pay him his fee after utilizing his services to purchase a house. On the day they met, the young man agreed to sign the listing agreement and went with the agent to see an apartment. Once he finished the tour, the young guy was surprised to learn that a post about the apartment had been floating around different websites and that he could have come across it on his own had he looked a bit more. As if that wasn't frustrating enough, he found out that his parents had seen the apartment a few weeks ago, but hadn't said anything because they decided it wasn't for him. The following day, the real estate agent received a call from the client saying that he wasn't interested in the apartment. A few months later, however, the agent found out, via the neighbors in the building, that the young man had gone ahead and bought it behind his back, without paying the agency fees.

Straight away, the agent filed a lawsuit against the young man who had purchased the apartment, circumventing paying the realtor's fee.

In his statement of defense, the young man pointed out several claims explaining why he wasn't obligated to pay the agent. For one, he insisted that his parents had seen the apartment several weeks before and that he would've bought the place anyhow without the help of the realtor. He also claimed that he had specifically asked the realtor to present only apartments that weren't posted online. All things considered, the young man announced that the realtor's role in the purchase of the apartment was minute and, therefore, undeserving of the fees.

In preparation for the case, I put myself in the young man's shoes. I tried to understand what would cause him to go behind the realtor's back despite signing the contract. I pictured the hardships young couples go through as they save up every last penny for their dream house. The loans they take, the debts they accumulate, and the infinite compromises they make in the hopes of one day owning a house. Particularly, I envisioned what it's like to spend a few minutes with a realtor, only to have him demand a ridiculous sum for a house I could have bought without his assistance. I tried to feel the frustration and anger of the young man, and the burning desire to escape the payment.

True enough, I felt angry for the thousands of dollars that could have been saved. I began to feel like an impulsive idiot for signing the contract when I could have purchased the property without paying the realtor a dime.

Putting myself in his shoes, I understood the man's desire to avoid paying the realtor, a greedy man who made a living off of young couples working terribly hard to save for a home.

By putting myself in his position, I was able to understand the rage he felt toward my client. When I met him in court afterward, I asked him pointed questions that resulted in just the type of answers I was looking for. Overall, the mood in the room wasn't hostile, but rather empathetic and understanding, as if I was talking to the young man on the couch in my living room. After a few introductory questions, I asked the defendant: "It must've been hard for you and your wife to come up with the money for the house, am I right?" The young man shared that they had a daughter and that they were working around the clock, still living with his parents so they could save every penny.

I asked: "It must have felt terrible to realize you had to pay the realtor money for an apartment you could have found on your own, one that your parents had already checked, right?" The defendant looked at me suspiciously, not knowing what to answer, perhaps worrying that he would say something that would harm his case. I continued: "Honestly, I can see why you didn't want to pay such a huge amount. We're talking about a sum worth several working months. Still, why do you think my client doesn't deserve to be paid for his hard work?" At that, the young man straightened his back and announced that the realtor hadn't worked hard to get him the apartment, that he could have purchased it without his help, that he hated the fact that he was fooled so easily. "It's not fair. More than that, it's absolutely ridiculous!"

"What did your parents say when you told them you had seen an apartment they'd checked out before?"

"I don't remember," the young man replied with his gaze to the floor. Surely, his parents felt uncomfortable about not having told him about the apartment. It must've put some strain on their relationship.

His frazzled response was precisely what I was after.

Throughout the hearing, I tried to shed light on the real reason why the defendant dodged the fee — he didn't want to come off as a total fool in front of his family. Suddenly, the rest of the young man's claims sounded like whiny complaints coming from a third-grader. Clearly, not wanting to look foolish wasn't a good enough reason to dodge a contract.

When I first started working on the case, I was appalled by the defendant's behavior. How dare he avoid a contract he willingly signed? However, if I hadn't put myself in his shoes, I wouldn't have been able to dig deep and excavate the true motives behind his behavior. I would have failed to ask the right questions, those that would get the judge to see the real picture and rule in my client's favor.

We need to remember that stepping into the other's shoes is a means to achieving our goal (in my case, winning the legal case). We must be careful not to empathize to the point where we deviate from what we first had in mind (for example, feeling so sorry for the defendant to the point of siding with him).

Whenever I step into someone else's shoes, whether it be my wife, a friend, a judge, or a client, I always discover new ways to act, avenues I hadn't previously thought of. In some cases, I'll try and get the person I'm speaking with to step into my shoes and develop empathy for my situation. This has the same boosting effect on persuasion. When both sides 'swap places,' reaching a mutual agreement becomes surprisingly easy.

Being Understood Means Being on the Same Side

When someone empathizes with our pain, a tight bond develops.

Picture this: upon returning home from work, you step inside with a solemn face and complain to your wife about the long hours and the horrible boss who's been working you overtime. Your partner glances at you with loving eyes and expresses complete understanding of your situation. At that moment, your emotions are granted a certain legitimacy. If not for her compassion, you would have felt much more frustrated.

Every person in this world longs to be heard without any judgement or criticism. We need to have our emotions legitimized, or else we might start to feel terribly confused or even crazy.

By siding with people, we're letting them know we acknowledge what they're going through. This display of compassion shows that we've been listening to their story, even if we don't necessarily agree with what is being said.

To be viewed as a 'friend' and not a 'foe,' we must first validate the other person's fears, no matter how we feel about them.

Let's say, for example, I want to convince someone to do something, but they express reluctance. It would be a horrible mistake to disregard the person's feelings and brush off their worries. This behavior is akin to someone confessing their deepest fear only to receive a slap to the face in return.

When people confide in us, we must listen and express empathy with phrases such as:

"I agree"

"I thought so too in the past"

"I did the same thing"

"I can relate to what you're saying"

Once we've expressed our sympathy, we can slowly divert back to our original stance and lay out our argument with an approachable tenderness.

It shouldn't be too hard to relate to the other. If you look deep enough, you can always find at least one thing on which you can agree. Even if you feel that things are far from your understanding, try to acknowledge the emotions behind the other person's behavior. Fear, anger, or joy, for example, are feelings we've all experienced before.

Our point of view is entirely subjective and, therefore, when we empathize with the other, we're simply acknowledging the sheer fact that what they feel is real to them.

When hearing phrases like "I agree" or "I thought so too in the past..." we automatically lower our guard and start viewing the person before us as a friend to whom we can relate.

If, during a court hearing, a judge tosses a question at me, it would be a mistake to say: "Your Honor, the question you just asked me is completely out of place. Looking at the evidence, it's obvious that my client has obeyed the law." Such a dismissing sentence can destroy any chance of the judge ruling in my client's favor. The better answer to his question would be: "I understand Your Honor's concerns, and the question you have posed is fitting. To be honest, I've asked myself that too but, at a second glance, I've discovered..." After validating the judge's concerns, it'll be much easier to express my point of view.

Mrs. Smith returns home one day to find her house turned upside down. Frustrated by the mess in the house, she's tempted to take it out on her teenage son, who has likely done nothing but play on the computer all day. The complaints come flying out of her mouth, as she demands that he clean his room this instant. To that, her kid will likely stare at the screen and ignore her. On the other hand, Mrs. Cohen can tell her son: "I know you just got back from school and you're not in the mood to do anything. Trust me, I'm exhausted, too. But a friend of yours is coming over today, and I want the house to be nice and tidy for the two of you." By validating her son's situation, she has made room for healthy communication.

Most attorneys seem to ignore the difficulties and troubles posed by the opposing lawyer. This shrilling indifference may get the judge to 'defend' the other attorney's stance, in the hopes of balancing out the energy in the room.

After relating with our audience, we must maintain that bond. Adding "but..." will wipe out every bit of empathy we expressed before.

Let's say a judge asks an attorney a question, and the attorney responds: "I understand your question, but that's not the case with my client..." As soon as 'but' is added to the equation, the former part of the sentence is canceled.

Instead of 'but' we can use the words 'that being said' or 'and.'

I have a good friend, also a lawyer, and every time I express my thoughts around him, he always responds to everyone with: "no," or "no, but..." Unbeknownst to him, he has canceled my opinion on the spot, even if he actually intended on agreeing with me.

If I tell him: "Wow, this winter has been dry..." He'll respond: "No, look, we're in desperate need of rain." The habit of starting every sentence with 'no' is characteristic of lawyers. They always feel like they need to hold their ground.

To steer people in our direction, we need to get them to feel like we're on the same side, and that we share the same interests. Initially, we'll relate to what they say and then, once we've found common ground, we'll open up and move forward with our genuine thoughts.

The Mere Exposure Effect
Research has shown that people prefer things they are

familiar with. The more frequently people are exposed to something, the more they prefer it. This is also true for ideas, values, beliefs, and opinions. The unknown is treated as an ambiguous and dangerous entity, raising suspicion whenever it creeps into our familiar bubble. In a world full of dangers, no wonder we stick to what we know. When it comes to persuasion, this notion must be taken into consideration. People's systems of belief are deeply ingrained and a comforting source from which they make sense of life. To take advantage of our familiarity bias, we can use phrases like: "You already know that..." or "Everyone knows that..." or "I don't need to tell you about..." These kinds of phrases will flatter your audience by implying how knowledgeable they are, as well as provide that sense of security that the ideas you are proposing aren't in contrast to their values.

When a salesperson for a real estate company wants to sell an apartment, he or she can tell the client: "As you already know, the market has hit a rough patch lately, and there's a lot of uncertainty regarding the future, particularly in stocks. But this gem of a property is just the right investment to grant you long-term financial security."

The salesperson kicks off his pitch by assuming that the client 'already knows' about the market's situation, then offers the client his initial idea: invest in this property and achieve long-term financial reassurance.

Note that the salesperson has pointed out an indisputable, objective fact: the market has hit a rough patch. Then, he offers a solution — invest in real estate. And while this isn't objectively the best way to go about it, it makes sense. By sticking these two pieces together, the client begins to view both parts of the phrase (both problem and solution) as objective facts.

As a result, the client will become less defensive, without feeling like they are being forced to agree with random, subjective opinions. After all, the salesperson has stated something they 'already know.' Naturally, this highly increases the chances that they'll be inclined to agree.

Set Up a Fan Group

When we like someone, we are automatically more suggestible to their offers. We're willing to give our loved ones — partners, children, or friends — nearly anything they want, just because we like them. When it comes to strangers, however, we become apprehensive.

As part of the research done at the University of California, participants were asked about unfamiliar details relating to famous figures. For example, they had to guess which of these options was right: "President Reagen scored a GPA of either 4 or 3." The results showed that people who liked Reagen attributed the higher score, while people who disliked him gave him the lower. Whether we're aware of it or not, we are forever entangled in our own subjectivity, heavily influenced by our personal preferences.

If I like someone, nearly all of my thoughts about them will be positive. As such, their words will appear more convincing, and their hold on me will be tenfold. At times, unbeknownst to us, we tend to go against our interests only because someone we like decides otherwise.

To influence others, we'll start by deepening our relationship to make them more comfortable around us.

Most people tend to overlook the importance of establishing good chemistry, assuming that people make decisions in a rational way. They believe that persuasion tactics alone are enough to make things move.

This is, of course, a mistake. At the end of the day, communication is the name of the game. If you've established a good, friendly connection with someone, you're already halfway in. On the flip side, if you aren't able to find any common ground between you and your audience, it will be harder to make an impact. There's no shortage of examples of top-notch salespeople with slick tongues who rely first and foremost on their impeccable talent to get people to like them.

Forming strong connections predicated on trust is worth much more than any sales strategy you'll learn in this book. Our ability to relate to our surroundings and become friendly with the people we meet, to the point in which they see us as trustworthy partners — is a skill we must learn in order to master the art of persuasion.

Nowadays, when we are glued to our screens, it's important to remind ourselves of the simple, yet powerful, impact of face-to-face interaction.

Several years ago, an acquaintance of mine invited me to speak in front of an audience who didn't know me. When calling me onto the stage, he announced: "I'd like to invite the author Tomer Sofer." With the spotlight on me, I felt quite awkward for being presented so vaguely. The audience had just come back from a break, and everyone was still either chatting or on their phones. It took about a minute of silence before the audience settled in. But the hall was filled with a weird air of discomfort. Once I had their attention, I confessed: "I'm sorry, I can't begin my talk as planned. I feel like we haven't been properly introduced, as if we're still strangers." My acquaintance quickly picked up on his mistake and rushed to the stage to present more background. Afterward, I loosened up: "Now that you know who I am, I feel more comfortable to start my talk." Just by providing a clearer picture of who I was, a bond was established, giving me the energy and motivation to deliver a successful speech.

When a person introduces us appropriately, either to a crowd or a single person — the first impression acts as a bridge connecting both parties. The feeling of familiarity and closeness provides a fertile ground for healthy communication. Conversely, if the presentation is sloppy — both sides will feel estranged.

Similarity-Attraction Theory

Whether we're willing to admit it or not, the person we love most is ourselves. That's why we're attracted to people with similar values and beliefs. They may even look like us.

When that happens, an instant bond is created, an unwritten contract stating: "This person reminds me of myself. They must be nice. I like them." This is an important point to address when it comes to persuasion, as it can be utilized in our favor. Similarities can be found in appearance, ethnicity, family status, hobbies, religion, past experiences, etc.

One great example of the similarity-attraction theory can be found in an experiment done by a researcher named Garner R (2005). Garner sent a survey to people's mails, but tweaked half of the names he used to sign off. Half of the participants received a mail with a name purposely modified to sound more like their own. For example, if the recipient's name was Sam Beckett, the author of the mail would be Samson Bennet. Kerner wanted to test whether the names would affect the questionnaire and sure enough, they did. The power of similarity worked its magic: 53% of the people from the first team (with the tweaked name) answered the questionnaire, compared to the second team's 30%, where the non-tweaked names appeared. As it turns out, all it takes is one little similarity to move mountains.

An entertaining field experiment regarding the role of similarity in society was published by Harvey Hornstein, Elisha Fisch, and Michael Holmes (1968), who scattered wallets around Manhattan along with a note stating the owner of the lost item's address. Half of the wallets belonged to a person with a common American name, written on the note in neat handwriting, while the other half had an immigrant's name jotted in sloppy handwriting. The results showed that the immigrant's wallet was returned only 33% of the time while the American's wallet, with a more familiar name, was returned a whopping 70% of the time.

People were easily convinced and acted morally when

it came to the belongings of someone similar to them, without knowing that the only reason behind this was the owner's name (and, perhaps, nationality).

In an attempt to land an internship after law school, I was interviewed by one of the top lawyers of an esteemed firm. I hadn't met him before and had no reason to assume we would have anything in common. I was a young, timid apprentice, at the start of my career, dressed in simple clothing. He was three times my age with flashy clothing and a confident stride. Initially, the interviewer asked me to introduce myself. A few seconds in, I threw in a word about my military experience and, as soon as I mentioned my unit, the interviewer's expression shifted. He leaned toward me, disowning whatever cold front he had previously displayed. Eyes wide with enthusiasm, he shared that he had once served in the same unit. Thus, in the middle of the interview, we began talking about our mutual experiences.

After a few minutes, the lawyer went back to asking me questions relevant to the role. Now, however, the overall mood in the room was much lighter. The formality between us had dissolved into a new friendship. I finished the interview confident that I would get the job and, sure enough, I did.

When trying to persuade someone, we should avoid discussing things we don't agree on. Discrepancies in opinions may cause unnecessary tension, barriers that will be hard to overcome. The more we emphasize our shared interests, the closer we will feel to each other.

When I first talk with someone, I automatically seek what we have in common. It can be a diploma on their wall that teaches me of a level of education we might have in common, or a book on their table that I've recently read. Even if I encounter a person who comes from an entirely different background, I can always find at least one thing in common — say, a stamp collection they've displayed, a hobby I might share as well. By bonding over this shared hobby, we can develop a strong tie that will override our different backgrounds. A passerby looking on would see us as two good friends enthusiastically discussing old stamps.

When talking with people, I become a detective on the lookout for shared interests. The stronger the interest, the tighter the bond. There is nothing like recalling sweet memories of a school we've both attended, or becoming passionate over a newspaper to which we've both recently subscribed.

If we want to perfect this skill, we should always do some background research on the person before meeting them — their hobbies, interests, education and past experiences. Keep in mind, though, coming off as stalking or creepy can ruin things, so be tactful about it.

Whenever I bring up shared topics, my client instantly views me as their equal. I become their mirror, and as mentioned before, there's no one we love more than ourselves.

When talking with people, I make sure to notice the language they use to express their ideas. I keep score of keywords they often use and use those same words myself.

For example, if someone uses the word 'great' quite often, I'll choose 'great' to fill in my sentences as well.

If, during a trial, the judge uses the word 'justice' as such: "I'll do whatever it takes to ensure that justice will prevail. After all, my decisions should allow me to sleep peacefully at night." A clever attorney will use that word to create the desired chemistry needed to help win the case. Using the word 'justice' to present their argument cleverly, they might say: "Your Honor, the arguments I put forward in the statement of claim prove, without a shadow of a doubt, that the complainant was harmed by the conduct of the defendant. Therefore, in order for justice to prevail, and for each of us to be able to sleep peacefully with the decision that will be given, it is best to accept my client's position, rule against the defendant and agree to the requested compensation." The judge, once they hear the same phrase they used prior to the attorney's claim, will unconsciously feel that the lawyer is speaking their language. With one simple word, a deep connection is established.

When Obama addressed the Egyptian citizens of Cairo in 2009, he was seeking to establish a bond with the Muslim world. Even though he spoke in English, he kicked off his speech with a greeting in Arabic: "Salaam Alaikum," and mentioned the Koran several times, thus drawing in several rounds of applause.

Many studies in social science have focused on couples, and for good reason. When examining the dynamics of people on dates, researchers have found that, on successful dates, people unconsciously mimic each other. If, for example, one partner put his or her hand on the table, the other followed. If one partner changed his or her sitting position — the other mirrored them shortly after. When people liked each other, they reflected the other's behavior, like a mirror. The coordination between the pairs included hand movements, blinking of the eyes, head nods, smiles, tone of voice, breathing rate and more.

They concluded that couples with good chemistry subconsciously sync their body language. Apart from the conscious exchange of words on topics like sports or movies, a subliminal dialogue was unfolding.

This incredible finding has deep repercussions when it comes to persuasion. If we actively sync our body language with that of our audience, we will be one step closer in winning them over. Our client will feel closer to us and grant us the access we need to get their support.

Let's say, for example, an employee is talking to his boss about a raise and, throughout the conversation, the boss' pace of speech remains slow and composed. To create the right chemistry, the employee should slow their speech to match their boss' pace. If, on the other hand, the employee babbles on relentlessly, tripping over his words and fidgeting in the chair, his boss won't feel in tune with the conversation. It will be as if the two are existing in separate worlds.

Mirroring our client can happen on several levels — similar language, tone of voice, body movements, facial expressions, eye contact, breathing and touch. As soon we master this skill — our clients will put their trust in us.

How to Make a Good First Impression

Before a flight, we normally go through scanning stages

at the airport to ensure that we're not carrying any dangerous items. If the scanning device detects keys or a cell phone, it will automatically start to beep, and the security guard will ask us to step aside and empty our pockets.

Much like a scanning device that sends an alarm of impending danger, each of us has a mechanism known as a 'first impressions detector,' an innate signaling device meant to warn us of sketchy people.

The gut reaction we get when seeing someone for the first time is a clever mechanism wired deeply into our brains. It's a rapid reaction, lacking any logical reasoning, that marks whether the person in front of us is good or bad. If the first impression we have of someone is negative, there's a higher chance we will keep our distance. Therefore, when it comes to persuasion, it's absolutely imperative to perfect our initial presentation.

The important sense of first impressions was developed thousands of years ago when humans lived in caves and the sole purpose of our existence was to survive. In such harsh living conditions, humans had to know, right off the bat, whether the person in front of them was their friend or foe.

Back then, there was little time to dissect every bit of the other's character. It was much smarter to rely on gut instinct to reach a decision. Any wasted time could cost them their lives.

Today, in the modern world, most of us aren't 'surviving,' in the traditional sense of the word. But we still possess the skills our ancestors had and often reach conclusive decisions on the spot.

This rapid mechanism doesn't always provide us with the full picture. There's a fair chance that, if we took the time to consider other factors, we'd reach a different verdict. But being as people don't invest much time in weighing the pros and cons, we should work to polish our first impression, as that is what people initially rely on.

At the start of my career, I attended an early morning hearing at a local district court. Back then, I was living far away and encountered an unexpected traffic jam which led to my late arrival. When I entered the courtroom panting, I learned that the hearing had started without me and the opposing lawyer had already begun discussing the case with the judge.

It was obvious to everyone in the room that the judge was angry at me for being late. The judge took it personally, viewing it as an insult to the judicial system. I was heavily scorned, like a third grader being yelled at for upsetting the teacher. All through the hearing, I could sense the bitter resentment coming from the judge, who was stubbornly refuting every claim I proposed. Eventually, they ruled against my client.

My bad first impression had a far-reaching impact. As it was obviously and painfully negative, whatever claims I made were futile. First impressions are made on the spot and have serious implications for the future. Sadly, we don't have a second chance to nail it. This slim window of opportunity means that we have to be aware of how we carry ourselves. We must avoid pulling any stunts that can harm our chances and, instead, focus on highlighting our strengths.

Forming a good first impression entails practice, practice, and more practice. If someone shows up to a job interview after hours of reciting their pitch at home, their first impression will surely be better than if they had slacked off and stumbled into the interview unprepared.

On one occasion, while representing a young couple in court, I waited for the judge to enter the room. Once her steps could be heard, I stood politely and waited for the hearing to commence. The judge ordered everyone to sit down. Without thinking twice, I stood back up and began to present my client's case. The judge, however, shot me a scrutinizing glance and said: "Attorney Sofer, where is your tie?"

I had been so preoccupied with the case that I forgot to put on a tie. Thankfully, it was stashed in my bag, and I could immediately adjust it around my neck. While most judges might've refrained from making a fuss over a tie, this one didn't. In fact, she was so distracted by my appearance that she couldn't focus until I put it on. Even though I tidied up my look, my first impression had been carved in stone and, from this point onward, the judge made sure to attack me at every opportunity. I left the courtroom feeling frazzled and ashamed.

If I come across a salesperson who is sloppily dressed or avoids making eye contact with me, my 'first impression detector' will start to beep. I'll wonder whether that person is hiding something. Perhaps their untidy appearance implies that they're not taking me seriously. Should I even buy their product if they don't bother to dress in the appropriate business attire? Our 'first impression detector' will produce a rapid, conclusory statement, resulting in something along the lines of: "There's something off about this person. I don't want anything to do with them." While the meeting itself may appear like it's going well (I might even smile and nod), I've already made up my mind. There is no way I'll buy the product, even if the salesperson happens to be a nice person who was just going through a rough day.

To form a good, first impression, we need to meet the other person's eyes and greet them with a calm, confident smile. We need to dress appropriately and articulate ourselves well. We should sit with our backs straight, and our hands resting calmly by our sides or on the table. Avoid nervous fidgeting.

There is no dodging the verdict of first impressions. They should be taken seriously, as that first moment is our springboard to the next step in the delicate process of effective persuasion.

What We Have is Mutual

Samples of buttery pastries are arranged in neat rows at the entrance to my local bakery. Their warm, freshly baked, yeasty smell and flaky texture entices everyone who walks by. There's no need to pay for a bite, and no one is obligated to buy one. People can come, try a piece, and go as they wish. One day, I walked past the bakery with my eldest son, who was six years old at the time. Surprised by the free gift, he peered at me innocently and asked: "Dad, how are they handing out cookies for free? Aren't they losing money?"

Of course, the bakery wasn't losing money for being generous. The idea is simple: after a client tries one of the pastries, they automatically feel obligated to 'return the favor.' I told my son that there was no need to worry about the bakery's profits. In fact, I said, the samples given out were there to lure people in and increase their clientele.

In this section, we'll discover a unique way of making people feel as if they 'owe us something' before we have even asked for it.

Let's say, for example, you go out on a hike. Suddenly, somewhere along the trail, you come across a person who has fallen into the nearby river and is yelling for help. Without thinking twice, you dive into the stream to save them. Right before they drown, you're able to pull them out. Such a person would be willing to do practically anything to return the favor.

While saving someone's life in the middle of a hike is rare, the sentiment of 'owing' something to another isn't.

Humans are social creatures. We live in communities and our sense of self is predicated on the way we're perceived by others. We put in a lot of effort into belonging. This is why reciprocity is so deeply ingrained in our system, at times causing us to do things we wouldn't have normally done.

Nearly all of us feel the need to respond to a kind deed with another kind deed. Most people find it hard to live with the lingering and taunting thought of owing something to someone. When it comes to persuasion, we can leverage that fact and use to it our advantage. Firstly, we should do someone a favor, something small. This way, our chances of receiving a "yes" will increase.

Throughout my life I've learned that a kind word, or lending a helping hand when needed, breeds positivity. Apart from spreading good in the world, I'm creating an underlying sense of urgency to the people I've helped.

One evening, on my way back from the office, I stopped by the traffic light and waited for the light to turn green. Suddenly, a 15-year-old kid pounced on my car and began to wipe the windshield clean. I waved my hands in the air and shot him a pretty clear expression that implied my lack of interest, which he blatantly ignored. After he finished, he stood by my window and smiled. Surely, the boy assumed I would feel that I owed him something for his services, however uninvited. Sure enough, without thinking twice, I handed him some coins. However, had he demanded payment, I wouldn't have given him a dime. But his timid expression and reserved smile paid off.

Street performers who play music or juggle for those passing by rely on the same effect of reciprocity, hoping that people will toss in some money for their show. In some restaurants, waiters will place a small piece of chocolate or candy with the bill in the hopes of boosting their tip.

These small gestures don't require much effort, only some attention. If we grant our client something, even if it's small, it will tap into their conscience and nudge them into giving us something in return. It can be an invitation to go out for lunch, a small gift like a calendar, a smile, or a simple compliment. We don't need to go crazy or spend thousands of dollars to incite the feeling of reciprocity.

That being said, we need to be wary of gestures that come off as bribes or pompous flattery. People can easily tell when we're being nice just to get something out of it. If that happens, we will immediately lose our credibility. Being gentle and honest is key. Remember to give from a place of authenticity, not selfish interest. A small, honest favor can breed a much larger one in return.

Covert Persuasion

One of the cleverest forms of persuasion is when it's done surreptitiously. This technique involves tactics to gently nudge people toward a decision. It has the power to overcome any uncertainty while drawing an extraordinary amount of sympathy from the crowd.

By persuading in a subtle, covert manner, our client has no idea they're being influenced, just as a patient under anesthesia doesn't know they're undergoing surgery.

The success rate of this technique proves that people are most persuaded when they don't feel like they're being persuaded. By influencing people in a way that doesn't reveal our intentions, our audience is more likely to adhere to our ideas, particularly because they have the sensation that they've come up with the idea themselves.

If I ask someone who has recently bought a product: "Who convinced you to buy it?" assuming they have been covertly persuaded, they will probably reply that they, themselves made the decision.

Let's imagine we're walking around the mall in search of hand cream when we suddenly overhear a couple gushing over a product that has left their hands as soft as velvet. After listening closely, the chance of us being persuaded by their enthusiasm, which wasn't purposely targeted toward us, is extraordinarily high. In contrast, picture a situation where you're walking around the mall when suddenly a salesperson pounces on you and starts babbling about a fantastic new hand cream. The reason why you're more likely to be persuaded in the former scene is simple: people prefer to have messages transmitted to them inadvertently rather than aggressively. The latter scene entails a straightforward interest by the salesperson who wants to profit off you, as opposed to the couple with no financial interest.

For that reason, if we're looking to sell a product, it's better to ask a third party (someone who isn't, supposedly, involved in the sale) to put out a generous review. Salespeople often market their products by posting videos of satisfied customers happily recommending them. Even if we suspect the videos are staged, we're still highly susceptible. When it comes to education, for example, parents have much more influence on their kids when they act as role models (a covert form of persuasion) as opposed to lecturing them directly on a topic.

Dan has recently moved to a new city and is searching online for a dentist to help relieve him of his aching tooth. Since Dan doesn't know any dentists in town, he calls one he finds through the Internet and schedules an appointment. Dan arrives at the clinic and sits in the waiting room. Suddenly, he overhears two patients praising the dentist and raving over his widely acclaimed reputation. On the walls of the room, Dan notices newspaper articles pointing out the doctor's achievements, along with praises and certificates attesting to the thorough training he has undergone.

After overhearing the patients' conversation and spotting the emblematic tokens on the walls (forms of covert persuasion), Dan is now much more convinced that this doctor was the right choice.

The intent of lawyers who appear in court is to directly persuade the judge to agree with them. They argue for hours on end, doing whatever they can to steer the judge's opinion in their direction. As opposed to a subtle, nuanced form of persuasion, this explicit attempt is exhausting. In my opinion, the best attorneys are those who can lay out their claims in a way that will cause the judge to feel as if they have reached the conclusion on his own.

It takes time to master the art of subtle convincing. It requires maximum precision, practice, and time until it becomes second nature to you.

The first step is knowing how to let go. Instead of trying to dominate the conversation, we should trust that people can choose what's best for themselves.

Sam, an attorney, met with a client at his office to discuss the cost of legal representation in a complex court hearing. Sam can sell himself to the client as follows: "Look, I have a Ph.D. in law as well as 15 years of experience representing citizens in lawsuits against the state. I've written numerous books and articles in this field.

Surely, I am the most suitable attorney for you in this case."

Many people who are trying to sell you their product or services will straightforwardly market themselves by showing off their certifications and stamps of approval. The problem with this is that it may come off as aggressive and off-putting.

On the other hand, Attorney Sam can opt for a subtler form of marketing:

"Do you see the paper I'm holding? We received this verdict yesterday from the Supreme Court. I've spent the past four years fighting for my client to get them well-deserved compensation from the state. Along with other cases I've won in the past 15 years, this verdict is yet more proof that it is worthwhile to fight against the state's oppression, even if it takes a while. Listen to this. About a year ago, I flew to a conference to give a lecture about lawsuits against the state. And guess who sat next to me on the plane? The Minister of Finance. The two of us spent the next hour or so talking about the state's problematic approach toward its innocent citizens. When the minister asked me what my thoughts were, I pulled out a copy of my second book called "State Police," based on my doctoral thesis from Harvard, and handed it to him as a gift. In the book, I discuss the unequal power relations between the state and its citizens when it comes to legal proceedings."

On the face of it, this is an ordinary conversation between an attorney and a potential client. By listening closely, however, several things can be extracted:

1. Attorney Sam has 15 years of experience in the field
2. Attorney Sam is a well-renowned lecturer
3. Attorney Sam hangs out with important people
4. Important people, like the Minister of Finance, are interested in Sam's opinions
5. Attorney Sam has written at least two books on the topic
6. Attorney Sam has a PhD from a coveted university
7. Attorney Sam has won many cases
8. Attorney Sam fights for his clients, even if it takes years

Armed with this information, the client will presumably conclude that Sam is the right attorney for them, and will decide to hire him. The decision, they assume, was theirs all along.

Another way I surreptitiously persuade people is by quoting others. I base my claim or idea on a well-known quote, using a phrase that strengthens my statement, but in a subtle way. People tend to agree with quotes they've heard before because they're attributed to the wise and famous. After all, if everyone has been quoting the same people time and again — their claims must be objectively true (this is, of course, false). Idioms like "Don't judge a book by its cover" or "A bird in the hand is worth two in the bush" are seen as indisputable truths. There's no arguing with the person quoting these sayings, as they're not the ones who came up with it in the first place.

Due to the impact of covert persuasion, many business owners hang 'objective' articles on their office walls written about them in the papers, as well as thank you letters from clients, or diplomas and certificates glorifying their level of education. They also tend to dress fashionably and drive lucrative cars. These implicit signs highlight the person's professionality and success, without them ever having to speak a word of it. Plainly stated, a person can either brag about being rich or cruise around the city in their Porche.

Questions as a Form of Covert Persuasion

One of the best ways to persuade someone without their noticing is by asking questions. Some people raise their brows when they hear me claim that questions alone can beat any sophisticated argument. But I assure you, once you adapt this technique, you'll realize how little effort is required to get results.

Just as the Pied Piper of Hamelin led the mice with the sound of his flute, our questions will lead our audience to the precise place we want them to be.

Finding the right questions requires a great deal of practice and patience. When we ask questions, we're acting against our instinct, which is to speak at length and control the conversation. But when done right, questions can lead our audience to the desired result.

Let's say Susan wants to convince her husband Mark to go on a trip to Italy. Being that their previous vacation in Italy was a disaster for Mark, Susan knows this will be a challenge.

For this seemingly impossible mission, Susan decides to take Mark out for a romantic dinner.

Susan: "Mark, you know, it's been a while since we

went on vacation. I'm feeling a bit overworked. How about we relax somewhere?!"

Mark: "Yes! I'm with you on that. Just pick a spot."

Glowing, Susan replies: "We'll be celebrating our tenth anniversary soon, how about a romantic trip to Italy? I've already spoken to a travel agent, and he has just the right deal for us. We'll plan it perfectly this time, so we can both have fun."

Mark made a face and sighed: "Susan, please, anywhere but Italy. I don't want to hear about that damn place. Do you remember what happened last time? I got really bad food poisoning on our first day at the hotel and then I broke my leg right before the trip ended. There's no way I'm going back."

From this point onward, the conversation heats up, and both sides grow evermore stubborn. Susan promises that things will be different this time, but Mark refuses to believe her. Susan doesn't give up and raises her voice, listing all of the wonderful things Italy has to offer. Finally, when Susan realizes that she's used up nearly all of her cards, she whips out the final blow, reminding Mark of all the things she's done for him, and all the times she has sacrificed just to keep him happy. She finishes by calling him an egoist who thinks only about himself. Mark slumps back in his chair and crosses his arms, further shutting down. By this point, Susan is raging. She's tossing insults and accusations his way. Mark defends himself from the barrage of fire being shot at him and shields himself by pointing out all of the sacrifices he has made for her. Ultimately, Susan fails to convince Mark to go to Italy, and they spend the rest of the night (and the following week) resenting and each other and hardly speaking.

People often choose to converse in this manner, and then wonder why they are not successful.

Just imagine what would've happened if Susan would've acted differently.

Had Susan asked her husband a few insightful questions instead of firing loads of criticism at him, while no one promises that would fully convince Mark, at the very least, she'd spare them a fight.

Susan: "Mark, my love, how about we go on a romantic vacation together to celebrate our ten-year anniversary? Just you and me?"

Mark: "That sounds wonderful. Now that you mention it, I really need a break."

Susan: "So, I have been thinking about a place... but please, keep an open mind about it, okay?"

Mark: "Susan, you know I'm open to things, but don't take me anywhere weird, okay?"

With a flirtatious wink, she replies: "You sure are. Say, how about Italy?"

Mark's expression freezes: "Not Italy again. I don't want to hear about that place. You know how much I suffered from the food poisoning and my broken leg."

Susan: "You said you'd keep an open mind. I'm sure you can think of at least one thing you liked about Italy, can't you?"

Mark: "There are so many other places to visit. Italy just... brings up bad memories."

Susan: "Do you remember the soccer game we watched at the stadium in Milano? Remind me... who played?"

Mark lets out a smile as he recalls the fun they had: "Oh, right. We watched Juventus F.C. play against Real Madrid in the Champions League. That was incredible. We also walked by the beach next to the hotel that night and watched some live music. Ahh, that was magical."

Susan: "You know I'm not a huge soccer fan. It was enough for me to just see you jump up and down like a kid. Remind me why that game was special?"

Mark: "It was a once-in-a-lifetime event. The whole world was watching! Two of the biggest soccer teams in the world played head-to-head. Actually, there's another Champions League game next month between Real Madrid and Milano. The winner goes to the finals."

Susan: "What do you say? How about we to and watch that game together? Do you know of any good deals that include a hotel?"

Mark: "Susan! You keep surprising me. I can't believe I might see that game live. It feels unreal! It's going to be one most momentous moments in the history of soccer. But do we have the money for it? It's expensive."

Susan: "We deserve it, Mark. We should be able to celebrate our tenth anniversary as we wish. Let's redo Italy, and make a better memory this time. We can catch the game and go to all of the places we missed. How does that sound?"

Mark: "I didn't know you were such a big soccer fan. I know of a site that offers vacation packages to include this game as well as a visit to Real Madrid's Museum. We can also go to the local bar by the hotel where all of the major fans celebrate after the game."

Susan: "Great. How about we plan the trip together this time, and choose locations we both like?"

Mark: "Yes, sounds amazing. We could really use a break, you know? Let's take a really romantic hotel and find the restaurants with the best food. No holding back this time!"

Susan's eyes soften as her lips curl into a playful smile: "This time, though, watch out for the rickety steps, okay?"

Mark chuckles: "Susan, you're really something, you know? You make me fall for you, again and again."

By asking smart, calculated questions, Susan has paved the way into Mark's heart and managed to get him on board to vacation in Italy.

Using aggression to convince someone is never a good choice. When it comes to couples, this can only lead to a pointless debate where both sides end up losing. Susan had no idea that soccer would be her ticket in, but by probing Mark with questions, she hit gold.

When we ask people questions, we're giving up some of our control of the situation, but we're still controlling the general direction of the talk. The answers people give us reflect their true needs, a point of reference from which we can come up with the right response. When you manage to convince someone through questions, the person will instinctively grant themselves credit for how the talk turned out. Ultimately, both sides will come out feeling satisfied.

But don't expect people to expose themselves so easily. Most people aren't even aware of their true motives and they'll often keep their thoughts, no matter how ambiguous, to themselves. By asking questions, though, we can help people understand what's going on in their minds. We can dig up their aspirations, needs, and weak spots.

The most important stage in conducting a legal proceeding is when the witnesses are called for questioning. At that point, questions are the only tools lawyers have at their disposal. During the interrogation, the attorney cannot make any decisive statements or mutter any unequivocal claims — only ask questions.

When in court, the questions I ask are like a projector meant to shed light on the opposing side's flaws. They are lethal weapons. One bad question from my end can lead to an answer that will harm my client and, perhaps, cost them the case. Conversely, a smart question will lead the witness right into my trap, taking me one step closer to victory.

It's important to note that the person asking the questions is subconsciously viewed as having authority over the situation, whether it is a doctor, attorney, psychologist or shop vendor. Picture a sick person who goes to the doctor complaining about some weird sensations in his stomach. Then, almost immediately, the doctor suggests a list of medications. Would you count on such a physician? If a doctor would recommend a course of treatment without asking you even one question about your situation, would you comply?

Isn't this what we're doing when we try and convince people without first asking them questions? We're handing them the 'prescription' without asking for any information.

In some cases, though, we need to know when to put a stop to our questions and get on with our goal.

A customer walks into a clothing store and, after a few minutes, picks up a blue shirt and asks the salesclerk: "Do you have this in pink?" To seal the deal, the right response would be: "Would you like to buy the pink shirt?" Once the customer says "yes," the employee should take the pink shirt straight to the checkout counter.

Some vendors, instead of asking the final, closing question to seal the deal, will add unnecessary doubts to the equation by suggesting more colors or other brands. If that happens, there's a higher chance that the customer will leave the store, overwhelmed and confused without having bought anything. A clever rule of thumb when it comes to 'closing questions' is to suggest two options and ask the customer to choose. Don't confuse them with more.

Let's say I want to schedule an appointment with a potential client. I'll ask: "Say, David, would you rather meet in my office tomorrow at three o'clock or nine?" Another option would be: "Do you want to meet tomorrow at my office or yours?" This question implies that the meeting is set for tomorrow. The only question is — where? Whatever he answers will be fine by me.

The goal is to make it easier for people to decide with the least amount of confusion. It's better to provide only two options instead of an endless list that may lead them astray.

Questions not only help us lead the other person to

our desired conclusion, but also make people feel like we respect them and genuinely care about their opinion. As a rule, most people are happy to have their wishes heard.

The Missing Piece of the Puzzle—
The Art of Listening

Using questions as a form of persuasion isn't worth much if you don't know how to listen. Questioning and listening are two sides of the same coin. They're part of the same skill you're trying to cultivate and perfect. After all, how can you ask clever questions if you're not paying attention to what's being said in return? Asking questions without listening is like throwing punches in the dark.

To master the art of effective listening, we want to make sure to get out of our heads.

Nearly every time I observe lawyers in court, I'm surprised to find out that most attorneys don't bother paying attention to what the other side has to say, including the judge.

Many lawyers, as well as nearly every person looking to persuade, toss aside the valuable information they've been given. And when they ultimately crash into a wall and face a dead end — they're surprised.

Anyone who is looking to impact others and win people over has to perfect the skill of effective listening. Unfortunately, most people are too self-centered. They believe that the pearls of wisdom coming out of their mouth are more worthy than the babble coming from the other side.

I have often stepped into court feeling fully prepared, with my arguments polished and smooth, at the ready to be whipped out when needed. However, when the moment of truth arrives, I notice that the judge isn't impressed by my claims at all. By paying attention to the shift in the judge's opinion, and by listening to his unsatisfied tone, I'm able to rethink my argument. Often, the claims I thought had little value ended up being the ones the judge found most impressive. If I'm not attuned to the 'flow' of the court hearing, I may find myself fixated on my claims just because I had rehearsed them multiple times before. Of course, such ignorance leads nowhere.

If I sincerely listen to the judge, a natural connection, predicated on respect and trust, will be established. This doesn't mean, of course, that I will back down whenever the judge begs to differ. I will, however, make it a point to stay flexible and adjust my claims according to our ongoing dialogue.

Everyone wants to be heard, and we can all agree that being ignored is a painful experience. Effective listening is a rare commodity nowadays, especially when our attention span has been reduced to a minimum after spending most of our time flipping through videos and photos on our screens at rapid speed.

If a couple yells at each other, for example, it's probably because both sides feel misunderstood. A person yells at their partner out of desperation; it is a cry to be heard.

It's important to understand that listening doesn't mean hearing the words coming out of the other's mouth. To truly understand the person in front of us, we need to pay attention to the whole package — their body language, their laugh, eye movements, tone of voice, the way they dress, and the way they walk.

Through effective listening, we can help people make the right decisions and achieve the intended results. By paying attention to people's stories, we're giving them a reason to respect us and put their guard down. The trust we've built allows for constructive, empowering conversations and grants us smoother access to the other person's thoughts and opinions.

PART 3

The
Message

Persuasive Storytelling

In the first part of this book, we discussed self-em-powerment as an essential element to achieving our goals. The second chapter established trust as another vital piece of the puzzle. Finally, in this chapter of the book, we will learn how to turn our ideas and arguments into an effective narrative that will captivate our listeners.

Our stories are composed of three main elements:

"Keys to Heaven" — our arguments and explanations

"Heavenly Language" — our words, phrases, body language and tone of voice

"Heavenly Tales" — our narrative

Keys to Heaven — Ways to Construct a Compelling Argument

Imagine that you're facing a large steel door. It is completely locked — no way to enter or exit. Behind it is a valuable treasure. To snatch it, you can either break in or climb to the nearest window and beg someone from the inside to open up. Both options are not ideal. Imagine, however, you come across a small key that easily grants you access to the coveted treasure.

To achieve our ideal life, we need a set of 'keys' that

will open every locked door and every closed heart. With such keys comes great responsibility.

The more diverse our set of keys, the more power we'll have on others and the less time and effort we'll need to put into convincing people.

The Simplicity Key

Plainly stated — we're not convincing heartless robots but, rather, humans with real feelings and profound experiences. Therefore, we'll refrain from using fancy language or complicated terms that will make us sound detached and cold.

Albert Einstein, the renowned genius, stated: "The definition of genius is taking the complex and making it simple." If we keep our arguments clean and relatable, we too will become geniuses of persuasion. This key acts as a 'persuasion enhancer,' making our words sound more alluring.

When someone uses simple language to explain complicated matters, either through examples or visualization, this instantly creates a sense of relief among the audience. They are left feeling overjoyed by the fact that they grasped what was being said. In contrast, when people talk incessantly, using obscure terminology, the crowd may feel despaired and frustrated, certainly more confused than they were at the start.

Unfortunately, many lawyers fall into the trap of fancy words. Targeting the judge's intellect, they add seemingly intellectual "'fluff' to their arguments, but end up ignoring the emotions, which are at the heart of the judge's decision. When lawyers present their arguments through a set of cold, rational facts — their claims end up feeling flat and lifeless.

This is how a standard lawyer usually argues in court: "It is certainly irrefutable that all parties involved are in unison that this is a grave and cardinal matter. As a result of deliberate and well-timed fraud committed by the defendant, the bank, my client has endured mental anguish that is not insignificant. In fact, to this very day, the plaintiff continues to suffer emotional distress and staggering financial difficulties."

Upon hearing lawyers enunciate such perfectly carved-out phrases, trial after trial, the judge starts to lose sense of the genuine emotions behind the fancy jargon.

This type of 'fancy talk' lacks the power and creativity to spark visualization, emotion, and urgency among the crowd — precisely the elements that motivate people to take action. This form of overly calculated and cold speech will fall on deaf ears.

When a lawyer appears in court, he must convey his case through simple, relatable words, so that the judge will be able to imagine the human story behind it.

For example:

"John Smith, a 70-year-old widow, drags his feet every evening from the bus stop all the way to his apartment, which is located on the fourth floor of a building with no elevator. By the time he's reached the top, he's heaving, panting, barely able to open the creaky door. When he enters, he is greeted by a pile of unpaid bills strewn on the kitchen table. The windows are shut and the room is freezing. Why? Because David can't pay for heating. David Levi is a tired, worn-out man without a penny to his name. Not a dime in his pocket. The bank stripped him of everything: his pride, hope, and any remnants of self-respect."

When we use a high vocabulary that lacks imagination, the listener will have to continuously pause in order to process our words and, by the time they've sorted things out, they will have forgotten or missed the point of the discussion. Naturally, their interest will evaporate. That is, of course, if they attempted to understand us in the first place. Many won't even try to decode our perplexing jargon.

No man has ever convinced his wife with the words: "My lady, without a shadow of a doubt, we are affiliated by love (and\or affection and\or any other tender emotion you can come up with). In light of this bond, and without detracting from the means available to me, I request (and/or demand and/or beg of you) to educate our child in a proper manner, including, but not limited to, the use of yelling and punishments as permitted by law for a child his age." It goes without saying, this form of speech sounds ridiculous. If so, why do many lawyers insist on presenting things this way?

In our fast-paced world, where we're constantly being bombarded by stimuli, people are in need of simple, cohesive explanations. Contrary to complicated terminology, simple, intelligible words are the key to our listener's hearts.

The Consistency Key

The word "yes" is undoubtedly the most comforting thing we can hear after we've asked for something. Just imagine the moment a woman says, "Yes, I do," to her loved one after he proposes marriage, or when a customer says "yes" and agrees to buy the product, or when a boss tells their employee "yes" for a raise, or when a teenager says "yes" to their mom after she has asked him to clean his room. 'Yes' is a word that creates an instant bond between both sides.

The 'consistency key' will help strengthen our arguments, clarify our explanations, and give us an overall boost of credibility, making us sound ten times more convincing. By using this, people will grant us the coveted "yes" with almost no hesitation whatsoever.

In a study conducted by psychologists Jonathan Freedman and Scott Fraser, "Compliance without pressure: The foot-in-the-door technique," published in the Journal of Personality and Social Psychology (1966), researchers knocked on the doors of private homes in California and asked them whether they'd be willing to put a huge sign in their yard that read: "Drive Carefully" and, in return, receive $100 a month. Only 17% of the tenants agreed. At the same time, another group of researchers approached other houses and asked them whether they were willing to place a large sign with the same phrase on the corner of their window facing the street for $10 a month. In this case, more than 80% of people agreed.

After a certain period, the researchers asked the latter

group of tenants (with the sign in the window) whether they would be willing to plant a huge sign on their front yard for $100 a month. To their surprise, 67% of the people agreed, in stark contrast to the initial situation that garnered only 17%.

What caused most of the tenants who agreed to place a small sign in their window to plonk down a bulky one afterward?

As it turns out, when a person takes a certain stance (for example, 'I agree to place helpful signs in my house'), they will take that same stance at a later date, even if that means tweaking their behavior (for example, by agreeing to a larger sign). The rationale is that people don't want to come off as incoherent and wobbly. Inconsistency is often frowned upon by society and can tarnish our reputation. A person whose actions don't follow a certain trail will come off as unstable, two-faced, and unreliable (did a certain politician come to mind?). Coherent people, however, come off as positive, stable, rational, and reliable.

When we come out with a statement, our brains will automatically view it as a commitment and will try to keep us on board with it. We are wired to maintain a stable train of thought and avoid any evidence of inconsistency.

For that reason, if we're aiming to master the art of persuasion, we need to prove to our audience that their compliance is in line with their past actions.

A lawyer once represented a doctor who had treated many terminal patients throughout his career. The poor physician complained of panic attacks and depression, insisting that his state of mind wouldn't allow him to keep working. The insurance company, unwilling to acknowledge the doctor's frail mental state, refused to provide his well-deserved compensation.

Before court hearings, it's recommended that attorneys find cases in which the participating judge ruled in a manner similar to the position of the client they are representing. In court, the attorney can then utilize the consistency argument as follows:

"Several months ago, your Honor, you came to a reasoned judgement in the case 11-14-1224 "Dr. Momo vs. Mimi Insurance Company," a case nearly identical to the one presently discussed, in which it was determined that the insurance company is obligated to pay the doctor compensation for emotional distress directly resulting from his work with critically ill patients."

The lawyer will then present a copy of the previous ruling to the judge and will pause in order to let his argument sink in. Normally in these instances, the judge will slowly nod in agreement.

The attorney will proceed as such: "Moreover, your Honor, in judgment No. 12-19-000 that you ruled on one year ago, you stated that the insurance company is obligated to compensate the young doctor for emotional damages caused after a patient died at his hands during surgery. The latter case concerned a young doctor, at the start of his career, who was unable to overcome the trauma he experienced after one specific case. Our current hearing concerns a veteran doctor, who has treated thousands of terminal patients and who, after decades of dedicated service, is no longer able to withstand the mental agony of treating patients who will soon after die."

Now, too, the attorney will present a copy of the ruling to the judge.

After having presented the previous rulings, the lawyer can use the consistency argument as such: "With all due respect, the matter in this case is in line with the previous rulings given by your Honor in recent years against insurance companies that have forsaken their role as protective shields. We have numerous documents testifying to the doctor's mental deterioration as a result of his difficult experiences after devotedly caring for terminally ill patients. I am not asking the insurance company for charity, but rather, to compel it to act according to its agreement with my client. As with previous cases you have handled, I ask the honorable judge to rule against the insurance company and urge them to provide compensation, as my client has, for decades, held up his side of the contract and has diligently made the required payments to the insurance company."

By presenting the judge with previous rulings on similar cases, the lawyer has triggered their need for consistency, thus encouraging them to provide the client with compensation, the same result as in former trials.

Two researchers from South Carolina conducted a study in which 300 coupons for a car wash were distributed. The participants were told that every time they washed their car, their coupon would be stamped and, by the time it was full, they would receive one free car wash.

Two types of coupons were handed out. One had eight boxes yet to be stamped and the other had ten, with two of the boxes already stamped. In other words, both coupons needed more eight stamps to get one free car wash.

Several months later, the researchers found out that only 19% of participants of the first group, who were handed the cards without the initial two stamps, accumulated all eight boxes and earned the freebie. For the other group, however, in which participants were handed cards with two initial boxes already stamped, a staggering 43% of participants finished the coupon and received their free car wash.

The researchers concluded that people are more likely to along with an offer when they are made to feel that they have already begun the process.

When our client has already taken a small step in our direction, it will be easier to get them to make a larger step afterward. If someone has purchased a simple, inexpensive product from us, there's a higher chance they will return at a later date to buy something more expensive. This is the reason why seasoned salesmen try to get their clients to buy something small and insignificant at first, followed by something bigger. In this regard, there is a sales technique stating that if the salesperson gets the customer to say the word "yes" several times during the conversation about things presumably unrelated to the product, once they suggest buying the product, the customer will tend to, once again, say "yes."

The Key of Fear
One of human being's strongest driving forces is fear. I personally don't know anyone who hasn't experienced

fear. Deep within us, countless anxieties and worries determine whether or not we will do something. We're even afraid of fear itself sometimes. Ultimately, this powerful feeling drives people to act.

Fear's most primal function is to help us survive the dangers of this world. Without fear, we wouldn't care much for our lives, and the human race would never have gotten this far. It's an ancient mechanism wired into us from the time when humans lived in caves and had to flee the dangers of predators, sustain raging climate, or combat enemies.

Nowadays, most of us aren't 'surviving' in that sense. We're no longer dwell in caves, and the chances of encountering a lion in the middle of the road are slim. Our brain, however, still uses fear to warn us of impending, looming perils.

When we spice up our arguments with a pinch of fear, we cook up a winning formula — an argument that can touch people most effectively. Once we tap into people's 'primal brain,' we can synchronize them with our goals and get them to act instinctively.

It's important to see the other side of the coin: if we manipulate people by taking advantage of their fears and planting triggering imagery into their minds, they will avoid us at all costs.

When it comes to political campaigns, fear is the go-to tactic. Getting the crowd panicked over important topics like economics or geo-political security is presumably the best way to influence people to vote for a certain party. A naïve candidate who relies on optimism alone will likely lose the elections.

For fear to have an effective impact, it is best to create a sense of urgency by convincing the crowd that what they fear might happen soon. Anything in the span of a few years will bore the audience. This explains why the dangers of climate change aren't enough to get everyone on board to change over to electric vehicles or recycle.

Short-term fear, on the other hand, works like magic. Volvos, for example, are sold at a relatively higher price compared to other cars simply because the company has emphasized high safety standards, providing customers with better protection in the case of a car accident and assuring their safety.

Companies that sell insurance policies also thrive on fear. Fear of losing one's own life, property, and future. A typical insurance agent will stress the strong possibility of an accident or illness, highlighting the importance of a pool of funds to keep you afloat. As the client, you envision this scary scenario and decide to insure your and your family's life and well-being in order to sleep well at night.

Judges use fear, too, as a way to get both sides to compromise. Picture two lawyers waiting in the courtroom for a hearing to begin. The judge steps into the room and flips through the case files, scrunching her face in disapproval. Upon realizing that this case might drag on for years, the judge, uninterested in spending hours attending boring hearings, decides to act quickly and turns to the prosecuting attorney with a host of menacing questions regarding their statement of claim. In response, the intimidated lawyer stutters in an attempt to explain, but the judge's unconvinced expression leaves them feeling desperate. "Unfortunately, in this stage of the hearing, I don't see how these issues can come to a satisfactory conclusion." As expected, the lawyer and their client now fear the despairing result awaiting them.

The judge then turns to the defendant's lawyer with the same questions, pointing out the numerous flaws she has found. "Listen, I believe you and your client are facing a long trial, and the outcome doesn't look too bright. Your client may lose a lot of money along the way, not to mention the hefty sum they'll have to pay the prosecuting attorney." In light of these words, the lawyer and client now feel utterly hopeless.

Just like that, everyone in court now feels slightly afraid. The judge is dreading this tiresome case, the defendant and prosecutor are scared of the impending outcome, and the attorneys are worried about the long and tedious way ahead of them. Then, in perfect timing, the judge whips out a solution, a compromise, and asks both sides to consider it. If one side shows the slightest reluctance, the judge scares them back into submission. Finally, both sides agree to the compromise, and everyone, including the judge, is happy with the result.

Of course, fear as a form of persuasion must be used subtly. People don't like being threatened, and you certainly shouldn't scare off your client. The most effective way to tap into someone's fear is by doing so covertly, quietly.

I once represented a young, physically disabled woman who was suing her insurance company. Her car, which was modified to suit her disability, was stolen, but her insurance refused to pay any compensation for the loss. Without her car, my client couldn't go anywhere.

Before the first hearing, the attorney representing the insurance company approached me and declared: "Listen, you can either settle for 65% of the compensation funds or drag your client into a long trial where maybe, just maybe, after several years, she'll receive the full amount. Of course, no one wants to see your client struggle without a car for so long."

Poking at my conscience, the opposing lawyer used fear as a form of getting me to drop the case. They did so covertly, hinting at a potential, dreadful outcome in which the insurance company will make my client's life miserable with a trial that will go on for years. The attorney was smart enough to use the words "no one wants to see..." creating a sense of common interest.

People's deeply ingrained fears are a tool that must be used with integrity, in a way that will eventually benefit the person, not harm them. Taking advantage of people's fears will only stir hostility and antagonism, expelling you from the paradise you are attempting to create.

The Key of Relativity
Before lifting their paintbrush, artists must choose what they want to draw, which colors to use, and which parts of the canvas will be emphasized or blurred, a process of fine-tuning that is essential to bring the painting to life.

In many aspects, persuasion takes after this form of calibration, using similar techniques to navigate the nuances of human interaction.

Picture an exhibition with two works of art hanging proudly on the wall. Both paintings show a house, a river, a bed of flowers and trees. Even though the components are the same, the drawings themselves are not. One drawing shows a large, impressive house surrounded by blooming flowers, and a river flowing in the distance between mountains. The other drawing shows a tempestuous river running along a snowy mountain, with tall trees towering along the sides and a faraway house in the distance. While both paintings include the same objects, the artists clearly had different ideas and perspectives when painting them.

In much the same way, when lawyers represent their clients in court, they must know how to 'paint' their client's narrative before the judge in a convincing manner. The attorney's 'canvas' must comprise facts, arguments, and information highlighting its strengths, as well as its weak spots. Eventually, the judge will rule in favor of the attorney who painted the most persuasive picture. The same goes for other aspects of our lives: we must learn how to paint a persuasive picture in the mind of the other.

As lawyers, for example, we might decide that the 'house' in our picture represents our client's strong points (e.g., our client is a sincere, honest man with years of charitable work to his name) and the 'river' contains our client's weak points (e.g., our client has misbehaved, and unintentionally harmed the defendant). The attorney representing the defendant will aim to paint the house in the center of the canvas, and the river somewhere in the distance.

By using the 'relativity key' we enlarge and minimize the facts of our story. Through words, analogies, arguments, tone of voice, and body language, we're able to either blur out or shed light on the information we have at hand. To enhance our strengths, we will use powerful words, a dramatic tone of voice, and slightly theatrical body gestures. The most persuasive people you know use this tool at every opportunity.

Salespeople looking to market a relatively expensive product will glorify the object so that the price will seem fair in return for what the person is getting.

Let's say a customer asks a salesperson: "How much for the watch?" If the salesperson immediately replies with "$5,000," it might come off as pricy. However, if the salesman first lays out the advantages of the watch (original product, lifetime warranty, numerous functions, a world-renowned brand, etc.) and only then exposes the price, the watch's price tag will suddenly appear to be more reasonable.

When a potential client first approaches me and asks: "What do you charge for your legal services?" I never respond with a price. First, I explain what my services entail and, only after I've made sure they understand the advantages of working with me, I state the amount. People are willing to pay a higher sum if they know they will be getting their money's worth.

For twenty years, a farmer made monthly payments to his insurance company in case an accident occurred on his farm. One morning, he woke up to discover that his vast field of sunflowers had been burned to the ground. The farmer's loss was estimated at $25,000. In the policy contract he had signed, there were several conditions that the farmer had to meet in order to receive compensation from the insurance company in the event of a disaster. The farmer met all the conditions set by the insurance company except for one: he had a single camera on his farm, not four, as required. As a result of this violation, the insurance company informed the farmer that it would not be paying him compensation for the destruction of his field.

If the farmer didn't receive any funds to repair the damage, his business would shut down for good. He would be forced to file for bankruptcy. Refusing to back down, the farmer hired a lawyer to get him the money he deserved. There is no arguing that the farmer hadn't installed all four cameras in the field, as noted in the policy agreement. This bit of information is, of course, the client's weak spot.

However, here are the farmer's strengths in the lawsuit:
1. The farmer had paid the insurance company each month for twenty years.
2. The farmer had followed the rest of the requirements, such as the use of fire retardants and other safety tools.
3. The camera installed was of high quality and placed at a strategic point that covered the whole field.

The insurance company's attorney dwelled on the carelessness of the stubborn farmer, who had violated an essential condition in the policy agreement by not using four cameras. The attorney presented countless papers reaffirming the benefit of having several cameras; they claimed that the cunning farmer had made small payments (compared to what is customary in other insurance companies) under the condition that he would install four cameras to significantly reduce the risk of an accident. Moreover, they argued that the amount of money the farmer had paid up until now, or the quality of the camera he used wasn't relevant. Bottom line — the farmer had violated a crucial part of the agreement and the damage inflicted on his farm was his responsibility. The insurance company's attorney downplayed the farmer's strengths in the case (while putting a friendly front, typical of lawyers representing insurance companies).

As a response, the attorney representing the farmer would have to paint an entirely different picture. The farmer's strengths would have to be emphasized in bold colors, while the setbacks of the case would be blurred somewhere in the background. The lawyer would go on about the twenty years' worth of payment, amounting to a huge amount, much more than the amount of the compensation. Afterward, the lawyer would bring up the fact that, during their many visits, none of the insurance agents who had dropped by bothered to mention anything about the lack of cameras. Moreover, they would argue that, in this specific case, more cameras wouldn't have necessarily saved the field from burning. According to the police, the fire was caused by a combination of malfunctioning pesticides with unusually hot weather. The lawyer would present the farmer's 'weak spots' as ridiculous and marginal, refuting any sense of justice.

With the use of body language, tone of voice, and choice of words, each lawyer will try to zoom into certain aspects of their picture and blur out others. Eventually, each painting will hit the judge differently.

To minimize or downplay a negative deed, we can use the words 'only' or 'just.' "I was just playing with my friends a little, that's all..." says the kid to his mom after she scowls him for not doing his homework. The kid uses a surprised tone of voice as if he is completely stunned by his mom's scornful attitude. The kid might also add another argument to downsize the gravity of his misdeed by saying: "Mom, I know you slack off at work, too. I heard you tell Dad!"

People make decisions according to the image they have in their heads. When painting a picture, we need to let certain colors shine, while dimming others. Start thinking like artists, and paint the life you long for accordingly.

The Key of Science

Science transmits an aura of accuracy and indisputable objectivity. After all, one cannot argue that one plus one isn't two, or that Einstein's theory of relativity is wrong. That is why many arguments and claims are predicated on science, research, studies, and statistics. These rational tools, when presented, have an immense impact on our decisions.

Just as salt, paprika, and pepper add depth and flavor to a dish, so can scientific facts when sprinkled carefully into arguments. By using the key of science, we add credibility and logic to our claims, boosting the degree to which we can be persuasive.

Picture a salesman trying to sell a new product for back pain. He might spend an hour going on about the medical wonders of the device but, even then, there may remain an inkling of doubt in the customer's mind. However, if the salesman mentions a recent study conducted by Stanford University proving the product's worth — chances are, the customer's doubts will probably dissipate.

The salesman can mention the study in the following way: "According to a survey done by Stanford University six months ago, 70% of the users reported that the device relieve their back pain. Another 10% noted that it somewhat relieved their pain. These numbers are pretty impressive, and prove, without a doubt, the effectiveness of this device."

Most customers who will hear about Standford's study will be convinced that this device can, at least, dramatically reduce back pain (even if they ultimately decide not to purchase it due to its costly price tag). The reason being that most of us don't have the tools or academic knowledge to doubt the scientific studies presented to us. Most of us would assume that this research, conducted at a prestigious university, should be blindly trusted.

It's important to keep in mind that science isn't the ultimate truth. Research data can often be tweaked, and biases intrude even in the most presumably neutral experiments, whose results are often manipulated to get a specific result.

When presented with an argument based on science, it's highly recommended that you examine it closely and ask questions to help you understand the topic in question. There is a joke about a statistician who once drowned in a lake with an average depth of 24 inches. This might be the correct data, but it contradicts our common sense and, therefore, comes off as silly.

If we want to test whether the study presented by the salesperson is valid, we will ask about the demography of the research group, facts about the participants' medical background, whether they used painkillers or other medicines or treatments in addition to the device, who it was that conducted the study, who funded it, why the device failed to help a substantial percentage of participants, what were the long-term effects of the usage, and more. Many questions can challenge whether the statistics proposed to us have any tangible meaning.

Remember, before we bolster our arguments with scientific facts, we must always conduct proper research, preparing ourselves with the pertinent knowledge to support our claims.

The Interest Key

Humans have a natural survival instinct, a resolute urge to stay alive. If aliens were to land on planet Earth, they would encounter a group of addicts, hooked on the pleasures of life. This unwavering passion to survive at all costs is imprinted on each and every cell of our human body.

The 'Interest Key' is undoubtedly the cleverest one on

our key chains, able to open even the most hermetically closed door. People will do nearly anything we say if we can prove to them that the outcome of what we're offering is mutually beneficial.

If we're being honest, most of us struggle to lift our heads out of our own little bubble and acknowledge other's needs. Naturally, we find it difficult to notice the multitude of worlds around us. But if we learn how to adopt the other's perspective and respect their beliefs and values — our persuasion skills will skyrocket.

A mother returns home from work and, without thinking twice, yells at her son: "Jacob, I don't see how you can live in this dump! Clean your room right now! All this mess is giving me a headache. I won't let your friends come over to watch the game tonight!" The mom is viewing the situation through her narrow lens, expressing her interest alone: a clean room and tidy home.

If the mom were to swap places with her son and see the world from his point of view, she would probably say: "Honey, can you please tidy up your room? Your friends are coming over tonight to watch the game. It'll be a shame if they decide not to come anymore because of all the mess." By accentuating her son's interest, she can convince him that cleaning his room would benefit his social life.

Arguments that tap into people's interests are a powerful, persuasive tool.

If you listen to how people express themselves, you'll instantly pick up on what they want and need. A husband who tells his wife: "I love you more than anything in the world. You make me the happiest man alive," adores his wife because she makes him feel better.

A lawyer who wants to increase his chances of winning a trial has to study the interests of the judge responsible for the ruling. A central interest, common to all judges, is to keep things short and simple. To save them hours of tedious work, many judges coerce both sides into an agreement right off the bat. The judge's interest is of paramount importance, and the representing lawyer must keep that in mind.

Another thing attorneys need to consider is the judge's reputation. This may sound surprising but, if the prosecutor and defendant fail to reach an agreement, forcing the judge to rule against one side, an appeal might be submitted against them. If the court of appeals decides to proceed with the request, the judge's status might take a hit. A judge whose rulings are constantly being reviewed could be deemed as not having 'proper judgment' skills.

An additional interest to consider in court is the judge's self-respect. If you've been to a few hearings, you've probably noticed that the judges' ego plays a significant role in the trial. Many lawyers lose cases simply because they have offended or upset the person in authority. Unfortunately, while the judge's top priority should be bringing justice home, 'justice' isn't a word you often hear in court. On several occasions, I've had to remind the judge to put aside intruding interests so that justice could be delivered to my client.

Judges also seek to call the shots on important and influential topics, promoting a certain agenda, as well as leaving a mark in their respective fields. When conducting their cases in court, lawyers must take into account the variety of these influential interests and learn to speak the judge's language.

Nevertheless, if we try to convince someone against their interest, we'll encounter nothing but resistance. Any argument, no matter how rational, will prove futile. To dodge this obstacle, we need to either show the person that our interests work together or suggest a better alternative to what they currently have in mind.

Internal interests we all have in common include: being heard, understood, acknowledged, respected, being part of something important, surrounding ourselves with positive people, receiving approval, being admired, in control, satisfied, secure, and validated. Feelings of excitement, harmony, and fulfillment are also strong motivators. Common external interests include money, a coveted job, a loving partner, flashy car. External interests are nothing but the manifestation of our inner needs.

To organize all of the information we have learned up until now, we need to create a map of interests. This map will help us motivate others by underlying their personal interests in the matter.

To create this map, the first step we will take is to write down the topic of persuasion. For example:

- A raise in salary
- Getting your kids to study harder
- Getting people to buy your products
- Bringing in a larger audience to your lectures
- Convincing your partner to agree to a summer house
- More confidence at work

At this stage, we will answer questions to see how our request can benefit our audience. It's better to have several answers. That way, we can start building a proper argument.

- What can my audience get out of this deal?
- How can this topic help my audience?
- What social, psychological, financial, or spiritual needs does this tap into?
- Which negative emotions will this help to diminish?
- Which positive emotions will this add to their lives?

Mapping out our audience's needs will help us understand them better.

For example, let's say we're interested in convincing a high schooler to study hard for their finals. To form a proper map of their interests, we'll label the topic of interest: 'Good Grades.'

Afterward, we'll answer questions similar to those we posed above and draw a line connecting them to our topic of persuasion:

- The child's self-esteem will grow
- The child will feel more satisfied, content, proud, and confident
- The child won't have to retake tests
- The child will be appreciated by his teachers, as well as family and friends
- The child's social status will rise
- The child will receiving driving lessons, paid for by his parents
- The child won't feel like a failure

- The child will be a role model for his younger siblings
- The child will feel like he can accomplish whatever he sets out to do
- Excelling in his finals will grant the child a sense of self-worth that can affect other aspects of his life
- In the future, the child will find it easier to land a respectable, well-paying job
- The child will be fulfilling his potential
- The child will get into a prestigious university and surround himself with others who excel
- The child will have more doors open to him
- Excelling in the finals will enrich the child's knowledge
- The parents will be disappointed if the child doesn't get good grades

In this way, we will keep adding more and more ideas, without necessarily taking into consideration ones that interest the child. After we've accumulated a satisfying amount of answers to our topic in question, we'll mark the ones we believe will influence the child's motivation the most. Finally, we'll construct our argument accordingly, planting these interests into the conversation as we go.

For example:
Dad: "David, I want to tell you a bit about when I was in high school, and how I dealt with the pressure of getting good grades. Actually... I haven't told this to anyone before, not even to your mom. I'd appreciate it if you kept it between us."

Son: "Of course Dad, your secret is safe with me."

Dad: "In high school, I was a shy kid with barely any confidence. I couldn't believe I could excel in school, or at life in general. For years, I hated myself. I was always jealous of kids who got good grades or were extremely popular. Whenever the teacher asked us questions in class, I'd waste way too much time considering whether to answer or not. I was terrified to raise my hand."

Son: "I can't imagine you being shy and awkward. You're managing a hospital now! You have hundreds of employees working for you."

Dad: "True, I honestly can't believe I've made it this far. But I wasn't always like this. If I had to mark the turning point in my life, it would be in the 10th grade, when I decided to put my all into studying. I once studied 10 hours straight for a test, morning to evening! Most of my friends went to the beach that day, but I stayed at home and studied. When it was time to take the finals, I nearly freaked out. I felt like there was no way I could do as well as the others. As it turns out, though, I was wrong. I aced the test. I got the highest score in the class! This grade gave me a confidence boost like never before. The kids in my class admired me. After that test, I kept studying hard. And it paid off. Suddenly, everyone wanted to be my friend. I began raising my hand in class and gradually became the most popular kid in my grade. My life completely turned around. My parents were so proud of me that they got me a brand-new bike. Not only was I more popular now, but my confidence skyrocketed. For the first time in my life I felt like I could do whatever I set my mind to. And, sure enough, I got into one of the most prestigious medical schools in the country. I even got a scholarship to fund my studies. Today, I manage a hospital and derive immense satisfaction from my work. It all started with that one decision in high school, one small shift that completely dictated the course my life would take."

In this conversation, the dad has planted several ideas that can surely tap into the boy's desires. For example, the need to be popular, to get into a good school, etc. The dad didn't criticize his kid, nor did he force him into doing anything. He simply laid out his own personal story.

By mapping out our audience's needs, we can build an effective argument and speak to them in a language that will press just the right buttons to get them into action.

The Key of Effort

There's a positive correlation between the level of effort people put into getting something and their level of appreciation towards it. The more effort we put into achieving something, the more we appreciate it.

Think of all of the goals you've had to work hard to achieve: an academic degree, raising kids, running a marathon, or getting hired to a senior position at work. Surely, you're proud of yourself for reaching those goals. If you hadn't put in all of that effort, you wouldn't have been as proud. People find it easier to spend money they randomly received, like a lottery prize, rather than money they worked hard for.

The effort one puts into something, or the suffering one had to go through to get it — makes that achievement much more appealing and important. Knowing this, we can motivate people by reminding them how hard they worked to get it.

Imagine you walk into a clothing store searching for a nice suit for a family event. When you enter the store, an employee approaches you and offers to help. You ask her to show you some flashy suits and, after thinking things over for a moment, she brings you a white suit with blue stripes, with pink fur at the tip of the sleeves. The suit looks good on the hanger but, after you try it on for yourself, you're not happy with how it sits on you. You ask the employee to hand you another one in a slightly larger size, a gold one with a large image of a purple fish with pink stripes embroidered into the fabric. A minute later, the employee returns with the suit in hand. You're happy with the design and try it on. After checking yourself out in the mirror, you're still unsure whether this is the right pick. You spend the next hour trying on suits, sending the employee on several trips to the stockroom. A second before the employee gives up, you look into the mirror and smile at the leopard-printed suit, the one with glimmering pink dots. This is the one. The exhausted employee can now let out a satisfied sigh of relief.

"By the way, how much is it?" you hesitantly ask. After hearing the price, you decide it's too expensive.

"Look, the suit is gorgeous, but the price is too high for me. I can't afford it." Disappointed, you return the suit and head toward the door. The store's employee shoots you a desperate look. After spending a full hour running back and forth for you, she doesn't want all that effort to go to waste.

Before you walk out, you tell the store clerk: "Listen, I'll take it if you could give me a 20% discount. It'll still be expensive, but a bit more affordable."

After all of the effort the clerk put into finding the right suit for you, there's a higher chance she'll agree to give you a discount.

On the flip side, imagine a scene where you enter a store, try on just one suit and, a moment later, ask for a discount. The chances you'll get it are lower because the store clerk barely put any effort into finding it for you.

In 1959, researchers Aronson E. and Mills J. tested the premise that people who worked hard to earn something tend to value it more. The researchers opened a course at the university and divided the course participants into three groups of women. The first group was admitted to the course immediately, without an admission test; the second group was admitted to the course after passing a simple written entrance exam; and the third group was made to try harder and take a difficult entrance exam that had complex questions, both written and oral. The course was intentionally made to be boring. In that way, they could test each group's reaction. After several weeks, the first two groups reported that the course was painfully boring, but the third group, who had to put more effort into getting accepted to the course, reported a higher interest in the course.

If we want to influence people, we must get them to 'sweat' or have them sacrifice something in return. That way, what we give won't be taken for granted. Parents who want their children to appreciate a coveted possession may first get them to work for it. A 15-year-old girl who works as a babysitter and saves every penny to put toward a new bike will appreciate it much more, as opposed to if she would have received it as a present.

One of my friends posted an online ad inviting business owners to a free lecture on marketing. Many business owners registered but, on the day of the event, the vast majority of people who had registered were a no-show. My friend explained to me that he had called some of the registrants who were absent to find out their reason, and each of them said that they had really wanted to attend, but a 'very important' matter had unexpectedly popped up on that exact day. It was much easier for people to come up with an excuse not to come to the lecture when it was free of charge. The next time my friend decided to market a lecture of his, he posted it for a nominal charge. Ultimately, most of the people who paid for the lecture attended it.

I believe that if we were born exceptionally smart and rich, with all of our needs already taken care of, we would experience life to be boring. We would have been floating around mindlessly, with no meaning. Life's imperfections are a gift from above and, thankfully, we have enough resources to make it perfect with our own two hands.

The Incentive Key

The 'Incentive Key' may seem trivial, but it is extremely powerful and can open a lot of doors in life. People often look at me funny when they hear me bring this up, but this simple shift in how we communicate can make a huge difference. The more we use this key in our day to day lives, the more doors will open up for us.

Let's start by pointing out people's affinity to do things they understand. Whenever there's a logical explanation behind something, people are far more eager to approach it. And vice versa. If something doesn't seem reasonable, people will shy away from it. This is why many people will agree to do something we ask, as long as the request is modest and makes sense. If we request something and pepper it with the words "because..." or "the reason is..." it'll be far easier to get them on board with us.

Researcher Ellen Langer conducted an experiment in which she sought to bypass people who were standing in line to copy documents in the library's printer. The experiment was divided into three parts: 1) The researcher asked to cut in line, adding a reasonable explanation to her request. 2) The researcher asked to cut in line but didn't explain why. 3) She asked to cut in line and gave a weak explanation for the urgency.

When given a strong explanation, for example, "Can I cut in line? My kid is waiting for me in the car," 94% of participants agreed.

When she asked to cut in line but gave no explanation, only 60% of people agreed. A drastic decline compared to the former result.

The surprising part was when she justified cutting in line by using a weak excuse, for example like: "Can I cut in line? I have to photocopy something," 93% of people agreed. This is nearly the same amount as the first scenario.

This study shows that even if we provide a weak excuse for our request, people will tend to agree. Our brains are wired to look for consistency and reasoning, regardless of the actual content given to us.

Naturally, if we can provide an explanation that benefits the other person, this will increase the chances of them complying even more. For example, if a mother wants her son to babysit his little sister: "Can you please watch over your sister tonight? I want to go shopping. I'll pick up your bike on the way." This request contains something of interest to her son — his bike.

Moreover, if we add 'cause and effect' to our argument or request, people will tend to agree with us. For example, by adding "If x, then y..." we're creating a logical pattern for people to follow, making it easier for them to accept our theory.

"If you eat fruits and vegetables — you'll be strong and healthy."

"If you study hard — you'll get good grades and be successful."

These types of sentences, which appear reasonable and logical due to their 'cause and effect' structure, have a greater effect on people.

The effectiveness of 'if/then' will increase dramatically if we insert, in the first part of the sentence, a fact that our listener blindly accepts and, in the second part, we insert a subjective assumption. Our listener will accept both parts of the sentence as true, because they have made the assumption that if the former part of the sentence was true, then the latter should be too.

In the examples below we will use the words 'If/then' to divide between cause and effect.

For example, I can approach my readers in the following manner: "If you have reached this far in the book (then) it is a sign that the topic of persuasion is very important to you, so you should continue reading until the end." The reason why this sentence makes sense to most of us is because the first part of the sentence is an indisputable fact — indeed, the reader has reached this part of the book. However, the second part of the sentence is a subjective assumption: "The topic of persuasion is very important to you," which is not necessarily true. The reader may be reading this book because they are bored, or because they need this for school. Ultimately, the structure of the sentence helps trick people into accepting the whole phrase as true, including the subjective assumption I planted in the last bit of the sentence.

Additional examples:
- "If you live in Tel Aviv (fact), (then) the municipality's corruption must interest you (subjective assumption). Therefore, it only makes sense that you join the protest next Monday."
- "Your Honor, if we filed a claim despite paying a fee of 12K (fact) (then) —this is a sign that the plaintiff was seriously harmed by the conduct of the defendant (subjective assumption), and therefore, our request must be accepted and the plaintiff's property seized (our request)."

When we ask people to do things for us, we must respect them by explaining the logic behind our request. It's best if we find an explanation that taps into their interests. Try and do so by formulating a sentence containing a fact. Your words will sink in much faster.

The Reputation Key

If you ask people what they think about themselves, they'll probably reply that they are good people. Viewing ourselves as a good and honest person helps us feel better about ourselves and life in general. After all, no one wants to go through life feeling evil.

When people lose in court, they often won't admit that they were wrong. Most of the time they will complain that the judge was biased, woke up cranky, didn't judge the situation appropriately, didn't read the files, was bribed, or failed to get to the root of the matter. All of these excuses are designed to save their reputation and sustain their image as people with integrity.

To survive in this world, we need to hold a positive image of ourselves, both in our own eyes and those of others. This fierce need of ours to constantly guard our reputation will help us when it comes to persuading others who share that same need.

A researcher by the name of T. Moriarty published an article in the Journal of Personality and Social Psychology (1975) regarding a study he conducted along with his two assistants. One of his assistants went to the beach and placed his towel and radio on the sand before going for a swim. After a few moments, the second assistant snuck in, snatched the radio, and ran off in front of spectators (participants of the study who were unaware they were being tested). 20% of the people who were at the beach yelled at the thief or tried to stop him. Most of the people, who felt that they weren't responsible and were innocent bystanders, didn't do anything.

The second experiment was similar to the first, only this time, the first research assistant asked the people on the shore to watch over his stuff. Now, when the 'thief' stole the radio, a whopping 95% of the people ran after him. Why? Because this time, they felt they had made a commitment and their reputation was, indeed, at risk.

Whenever I speak with lawyers on behalf of my clients, I immediately bring up the importance of integrity and fairness.

"I'm happy that we can negotiate in a fair and respectful manner. I don't know you personally, but I've heard from several acquaintances that you are a fair and open-minded person."

By using these words, I've encouraged the opposing lawyer to justify the compliment I gave him later on in the hearing.

I once represented a young couple who purchased a new apartment from a large contractor. Before the couple entered the apartment, unexpected defects and damages were discovered. The young couple brought me into the negotiation discussions with the contractor after much conflict, anger, and bitterness. The deal with the contractor was on the verge of exploding, moments before mutual claims were submitted to the court. A year earlier, I represented an elderly couple who were in the process of buying a home from the exact same contractor, and fortunately, that transaction went smoothly. At the time, the contractor seemed like a generous, decent person, and we managed to reach agreements acceptable to both sides. This time, I told the young couple that I already knew the contractor and that it wasn't difficult to reach an agreement with him last time. My clients thought I was confusing their contractor with another, and swore that this guy was a conniving liar.

We scheduled a meeting with the contractor in the hopes of reaching some form of compromise. A few minutes before the meeting began, I ran into him in the kitchen. We started to talk, and I brought up the last time we negotiated. I mentioned that he gave off the impression of being a good and honest man. Before we walked out, I told him that I fully believed that this time, too, we would reach an agreement. "I always keep my word," he muttered as we headed to his office.

When I entered the conference room, my clients were already seated at the table across from the contractor and his lawyer. As we went over the damages caused to the apartment, my clients were surprised to see that the contractor was listening attentively to what I had to say. He was even offering creative solutions to the problems posed. In the end, we managed to reach a wonderful agreement. The contractor behaved decently throughout the whole process and acted in accordance with the image I had of him following our conversation earlier in the kitchen.

People usually won't lie to us if we bring up topics like honesty and reliability beforehand. Studies have shown that people tend to lie less when they look at themselves in the mirror. I believe that says a lot about the influence of our self-image on our moral behavior.

When I want to get my child to clean the house, for example, I preface my request by telling him that I trust him to do it in the best way possible, because I know he is a hard-working and determined kid.

To influence people, we should make them think that behaving in a certain way will benefit their reputation.

The Authority Key

Those of us who are fortunate enough to live in a democratic society with full freedom of speech are able to share our opinions on whichever topic springs to mind. Simply by writing a post or uploading a video, we can spread our word across the Internet's infinite stream of meaningless junk. This results in cheap and, at times, fake, information with no real value. Every other person is an expert in politics, a seasoned psychologist, a spiritual guru, or a general advisor.

Now, more than ever, we appreciate people who have genuine expertise in their field. When an expert with a renowned reputation shares their thoughts, we take it to be true. We are far more influenced by people with the impressive credentials and positive reviews.

One day, when I was serving as a reservist in the military, I overheard another soldier sharing details about a dispute in his family involving an inheritance. I was wearing a uniform, so the soldier couldn't possibly know that I was a lawyer and I decided not to share my profession. Instead, I wanted to test how much power authority had when it came to persuasion. When I first stated my opinions, he didn't seem too impressed and refuted my claims by saying that he had friends who knew better.

When we finished the discussion, I decided to reveal my profession as a lawyer and told him that I had recently dealt with a similar case. At that moment, every speck of doubt he had expressed earlier had vanished, and he was now all ears. The moment he viewed me as an expert on the topic, every piece of advice I gave him made sense.

If we see a person on a TV commercial wearing a white doctor's uniform, and he advises us to take a particular pill, we automatically feel as if he knows what he's talking about (even though he's probably an actor). Interestingly, according to studies done on the topic, even if the commercial explicitly states that the 'doctor' is an actor, people will still be more influenced by his words.

In 1961, a professor of psychology at Yale University, Stanley Milgram, conducted an experiment to test whether an expert or an authoritative figure would be able to influence students to do things they wouldn't normally think of doing, for example, electrocuting people to a degree of unimaginable pain. In the study, the students were asked by a figure who appeared authoritative to gradually electrocute a person sitting in the next room. The volts ranged from 15-450. As it turns out, 65% of the students agreed to climb up to 450 volts, a shock strong enough to kill a person.

The 'authority key' is so powerful that the students in the experiment were willing to practically kill a person they didn't know, just because a respected professor ordered them to do so, even if it went against their beliefs. So many horrific acts have been committed throughout human history just because of someone who was revered and labeled as having authority influenced people to go against their basic goodwill and morality, and perpetrate murder, robbery, and other vicious crimes.

This is why in the 'Grand Sanhedrin,' an ancient Jewish high court, it was customary for the head of the court to hear the opinions of the newer judges first, and only then express his. If the head of the Sanhedrin, who was considered the most respected judge, had given his opinion at the start of the legal hearing, his opinion would presumably have influenced the junior judges, who would have been too intimidated to share their genuine thoughts.

People display certificates, diplomas, or newspaper articles on the walls of their office as objective testimonies of their skills and abilities.

If we want to influence people in a field that we don't know much about — we should seek information from people who we consider experts in that field. It can be findings from studies and books we come across, or any form of credible proof that can strengthen our arguments and cancel out any doubts or criticism.

You don't need to be an expert in nutrition to reference the world's most renowned nutrition researchers or enjoy some of their authoritative aura.

A few years ago, I was sitting in a cafe with a good

friend who was complaining about how the hospitality sector, in which he worked, was declining. After hearing him out, I gave him some practical advice, which I believed could help him stabilize his income. He didn't seem very convinced and practically dismissed every piece of advice I gave him. By the end of our talk, my friend told me had an appointment scheduled for tomorrow with a business consultant, an expert in the field. Several weeks later, I met with that same friend. This time, he gushed over the incredible talk he had with the business consultant and the noteworthy advice he gave. In truth, the advice given to my friend was very similar to what I had said a few weeks earlier, but I didn't want to spoil his enthusiasm, so I listened attentively and nodded.

When the advice came from me, a person who wasn't a business consultant, my words weren't as convincing. But when an expert in the field gave the same advice, my friend was willing to listen.

To create that sense of authority, we will normally present our level of education and experience in the field. We'll use jargon specific to our profession, clothing that suits our job, or other lucrative objects like cars and fancy furniture, just so we could exude an air of success.

To appear more authoritative, we need to answer the question: why should people listen to us in the first place?

The answer to this question will help us find the sources of authority and expertise in the field we are seeking to influence.

It is nearly impossible to advise people in the field of

marriage if you have been divorced four times and have failed to sustain a healthy marriage for more than three months. Similarly, it's impossible to influence people in the field of nutrition if you're a heavy smoker and overweight.

Remember to ask yourself — why would someone listen to me?

That way, you can reexamine your behavior, and strive to attain the knowledge that will strengthen your credibility.

The Shortage Key

"Survive, survive, survive" — that is the eternal motto of our primal brains which see our survival as the only goal that must be achieved at any cost. In our brains, we be good resources vanish faster because everyone wants a bite of them. For that reason, we must fight hard over things that are in short supply. Nowadays, even if that thing isn't necessary for our survival, we'll appreciate it much more if it's a limited product.

Let's say you are surfing on the Internet and, suddenly, an advertisement pops up inviting you to buy a ticket for a concert by your favorite singer. "Only 1,000 tickets left for the best show of the summer. Book your tickets now so you don't miss out. The sale is available for one week or until the tickets are sold out."

After reading the ad, you start to get a bit nervous. You surely don't want to miss the 'show of the summer,' especially if there are 'only 1,000 tickets left.' By now, your brain has likely signaled in desperation: "Buy a ticket to the show now, or else it will be too late." Once you start feeling anxious, you'll likely enter your credit card details and make the purchase.

Picture this: You're at your local grocery store. You head straight to the cheese aisle, where the vendor walks up to you and says: "Hi, which cheese would you like to buy?" You glance at the selection and pick out your favorite. If the vendor were to say: "Hi, which cheese would you like to buy? Oh, just so you know, we're almost out of mozzarella," the fact that there isn't much left of that particular cheese will increase your urge to buy it. If they're almost out of it, that means that many people bought it, which means that it's probably a good product.

As you read these lines, you may think to yourself: "What? There's no way I'd fall for that. I'm a rational person." However, when it comes down to it, studies have shown that when people feel as if something is about to run out, they will automatically attribute good qualities to that thing, and presumably buy it.

To combat such influence, you need to consciously talk yourself out of it; in this case, the mozzarella. Remind yourself of the cheese you came to buy in the first place, and if your heart desires mozzarella later on, you can buy it elsewhere.

Many commercials thrive off of these tactics:
- "The offer expires at the end of the month."
- "Offer valid while stock lasts."
- "Final week of the sale."
- "First 100 buyers will receive an additional discount and valuable gift."

These sentences ignite an immediate sense of urgency among buyers.

When we put out a profitable offer, we should mention that the offer is valid for a limited period of time. This way, we can get people to understand that the offer is a good one, and will expire after a certain amount of time. If we decide to use the 'shortage key,' we need to keep our promise and stick to our timetables, or else we'll lose our credibility.

A person who receives the unfortunate news that he is terminally ill and that he doesn't have much time left will appreciate the small, mundane things of life much more than when he believed he had all of the time in the world. The term 'mid-life crisis' was brought about specifically because of that sudden realization, that one's time on Earth is limited.

On one occasion I represented a businessman who served as a mediator for a real estate transaction but didn't receive any commission for it. I submitted a piece of evidence to the court, a recording that supported my client's position. The opposing lawyer objected to the recording and requested to disqualify it. According to him, it violated all sorts of technical claims. The judge listened to the recording and eventually decided to disqualify it.

Of course, I believed that the judge's decision was wrong because I knew that it was a piece of evidence that could help the judge reach the right verdict. But even though the judge canceled it, he still had to listen to it to decide whether it was presentable. Moreover, the fact that the opposing lawyer was against the recording made it all the more appealing. The stronger the lawyer opposed the recording, the more the judge wanted to hear it. Eventually, it influenced the final verdict.

Surely, you've heard of cases in which the court imposes a gag order, prohibiting the publication of a name, usually of someone famous, suspected of committing a serious felony.

The fact that the court refuses to publish the name makes it worse because now the public becomes ridiculously desperate to know who the suspect is. Rumors spread like wildfire on the Internet as every other person tries to find out the celebrity's identity. Eventually, the name is leaked and everyone talks about it for days. If, at the beginning of the story, the famous person had agreed to come forward, the ruckus wouldn't have escalated to that extent. People would talk, of course, but it would die down very quickly.

At times, I have presented my arguments to people and faced multiple rejections. When all of my claims are exhausted, I whip out the 'doomsday weapon' and, contrary to what is expected of me, I convince the other person that my product or idea is probably not suitable for them and, therefore, I wouldn't even want to sell it to them.

As soon as I tell my clients that my service isn't really for them, they want it much more. By creating a sense of shortage, of an offer that will soon expire, I have increased their urge for it. At that point, they will usually try and convince me otherwise: "You know what? I think your service is just what I need."

A product, object, or idea we are forbidden to use or

follow — increases our desire for it. Remember, people don't like to be restricted or kept away from things. Next time you try and convince someone, use this key.

The Key of the Herds

In 1951, researcher and social psychologist Solomon Asch ran a conformity study to see if individuals will conform to the social pressure of a group. He had seven people in a room do a simple task. Out of the seven, six knew they were part of an experiment, but one person had no clue. They were shown three lines next to each other, along with a fourth one presented separately. Their job was to figure out which of the three lines most resembled the solo one. The participants took turns responding, with the subject of the study consistently being questioned second to last. Consequently, he heard the answers from the five individuals who preceded him. In the initial two rounds of the experiment, all participants provided the correct response. Afterward, the collaborators shifted to offering the correct answer only in 25% of instances, providing an incorrect response for the remainder of the time. The goal of the study was to test whether the participant who was unaware of the experiment would change his answers after hearing the people who purposely gave wrong estimations. The results were startling. In cases where all collaborators responded correctly, the subject in question did so as well, without any errors. However, when the collaborators intentionally gave incorrect answers, most people tended to follow and give incorrect responses, too. Only 25% of the subjects deviated from the group's behavior and answered correctly.

Following the experiment, the researchers asked the participants to explain why they gave a wrong answer. Most people admitted that they were aware that they were giving inaccurate responses, but still chose to align with the responses of the group. Some subjects confessed to feeling uncertain about their judgment abilities, while others genuinely believed that their incorrect response was actually correct.

If, in a relatively simple experiment, most of the subjects veered off course and succumbed to the group's opinion, it only makes sense that the same kind of behavior would appear in more complex situations.

Consider a social gathering where we hear a joke that doesn't genuinely amuse us, yet we end up laughing because the rest of the crowd seems to enjoy it. In comedy shows, producers incorporate 'staged laughter' after each joke, all in order to get us to laugh at home.

We are inherently social beings who perpetually mix with different crowds. Naturally, our actions and thoughts are constantly being influenced by the social groups we hang out with or aspire to join. When we encounter dilemmas about how to behave, we often follow the herd, almost blindly. The underlying assumption is that if everyone shares a particular mindset, it must be the right one.

Picture yourself standing between two cafes, wondering which one to enter. The first one is packed, with a long line of people eagerly waiting to order. The second one is fairly empty. Naturally, you will be inclined to join the crowded spot. Surely, there's a reason why most people prefer it, right?

Cleverly taking advantage of this line of thought, a salesperson might convince someone to buy a cellphone by saying, "Everyone has moved on to this version." It's hard to resist following the herd, and salespeople know that well.

A mother might ask her son at the dinner table, "Why haven't you considered getting married? All your friends have done it. You seem to be the only one not getting on with your life."

At school, you may hear phrases like, "You should go to that concert, everyone else has already gone and seen them."

By using these kinds of sentences, we guide our listeners into believing they should do as others have done.

People aspire to be part of the crowd in order to feel secure and accepted. No one wants to feel left behind. Thus, for scenarios where the majority support our stance, we can leverage this influence to persuade others that our approach, aligned with the majority, is the right path for them.

The Key of Logic

It seems logical to use logic as a form of persuasion, right? The key of logic helps us convince even the most stubborn. When we encounter responses such as, "What you're saying makes sense," we know we have convinced the listener.

Logic is an irrefutable force that can't be overlooked.

It's a potent weapon in our arsenal, but one we should use wisely.

When I represent my clients in the courtroom, I use logic to navigate through obstacles, taking advantage of people's need for 'things to make sense' in order to win the trial. Similarly, in other areas of life, where logic supports my position, I will pluck on it like a guitar, and create an irresistible melody that will captivate anyone who hears it.

That being said, logic can sometimes sabotage an argument. For example, cases in which rational thinking leads to an unjust or immoral result, as happens in politics. When cold, logical thinking causes harm someone, the argument will fall flat, no matter how much it 'makes sense.'

When court rulings rely solely on logic but fail to deliver justice or express any compassion toward the delicate situation, they can ruin the lives of innocent people.

Using a logical approach in my arguments can, at times, clash with spontaneity, creativity, and vitality — elements that are crucial in establishing a charismatic discourse. Logic often comes off as dull and rigid. Consider, for example, an economics professor on TV discussing the logic behind investing. His words may sound so bland that you might even flip to a different channel. Nevertheless, it's important not to dismiss logic off the bat. A creative mind can find a way to blend logic into their arguments.

Before we use logic to convince others, we need to understand a fundamental principle: what makes sense to me may not necessarily make sense to others. Relying solely on logic-based arguments can be dangerous. Individuals who use logic alone often fail to create a genuine connection with the other.

I once knew a smart lawyer who had plenty of experience under his belt. For some reason, though, he lost many trials. Engaging in any debate with him, whether about law or the weather, proved futile, as he would never change his opinion. Any attempt to challenge this brilliant lawyer's opinions was met with stubborn replies, all founded on logic and rational thinking. But his reliance on logic alone resulted in numerous defeats in court. During lunch one day, he spoke about a case he was handling and shared his exceptionally logical argument. I told him that, even though his claims seemed reasonable, I still wouldn't have ruled in his favor. A while later, I found out that he had lost (as expected) because the judge couldn't connect with his arguments as they were clearly harming the other side.

If you base your position solely on logic, know that you can also fall because of that same logic. This key is a double-edged sword and, therefore, it should be wielded with the necessary caution; otherwise, you may end up injuring yourself with your blade.

Rational arguments may be predicated on some fundamental principle we have, but others may not share that same perspective. When persuading others, we should strive to get them to agree with our logic. Remember to be creative and flexible, as our perspectives may differ from how others see things.

The Justice Key

Notions of justice or injustice possess a considerable influence on an argument and can inspire people to take action. Individuals may go to great lengths — violate laws, defy the government, and pay whatever cost is necessary to ensure that their sense of justice prevails. Throughout history, people have sacrificed their lives, endured lengthy prison sentences, acted against their own self-interest, and sustained significant damage for the sake of getting things right.

Dr. Martin Luther King, Jr. convinced the masses in America to advocate for the human rights of the African-American community. He addressed the issues of injustice and inequality without resorting to violence. His famous statement captures the impact of the notion of justice: "I believe that unarmed truth and unconditional love will have the final word in reality. This is why right, temporarily defeated, is stronger than evil triumphant." The 'Key of Justice' that Dr. King used brought about a transformative shift in America, sparking a genuine revolution in global human rights.

When possible, we will incorporate justice, or injustice, into our arguments. The Key of Justice works like a strong turbo engine, capable of penetrating the hearts of even the most indifferent individuals and motivating them to act with minimal resistance.

The justice argument speaks to the hearts of people but, to complement the sentiment we have elicited, we will add rational explanations to back it up. A combination of justice and logic will wield a significantly greater influence on people.

For the most part, notions of injustice may be absent in our daily conversations, and the focus may lean more toward common interests. However, the moment we encounter a point of injustice, we normally protest against it. We criticize any lack of justice, oppression, persecution, assault, discrimination, theft, or harm to the weak. Unjust actions ignite an immediate unease, plunging us into a storm of emotions and a powerful urge to take action here and now.

If a politician presents logical and compelling arguments in support of an oppressing law, an unjust, discriminating, and harmful one, the masses will normally take to the streets and protest against it. The seemingly logical law will appear dull and flat next to the humanistic aspirations of those protesting against it.

When parents treat their kids differently, favoring one sibling over another without any explanation, feelings of resentment will surely sprout.

Lawyers frequently encounter tired, grumpy judges in court. The judge's sour attitude causes them to be extra hostile and impatient toward anyone who comes before them. For this reason, in those cases lawyers must soften the judge's heart by emphasizing the value of justice. If not, their client may lose.

In such cases, an attorney can present their argument in the following way: "Your honor, I recognize your duty to uphold the law in this courtroom. Regrettably, it's not uncommon for my colleagues to mislead and challenge your rightful perspective. While most precedents may not favor our case, justice stands on our side. A successful judgment, after all, is the embodiment of justice. Let me explain why my client is deserving of justice." Following this introduction, the attorney will narrate the client's story, highlighting the injustice that has occurred.

When faced with a closed heart, the justice key can unlock it and bring about meaningful change.

Heavenly Language

In the earlier sections of the book, we explored a variety of 'Keys to Heaven' designed to enhance motivation in others and effectively persuade them to fulfill our requests. The keychain currently in our possession holds compelling tools that can unlock any closed door and exert influence on those around us. However, there will be instances that require more refined communicative tools. In these cases, precision in language and communication becomes crucial for delving into people's emotions and inspiring them to reconsider their perspectives.

The 'keys to heaven' are like tanks, fighter planes, and missiles, conducting overt and direct assaults on enemy targets. In contrast, 'heavenly language' encompasses cyber, guerilla, and intelligence units operating discreetly and precisely beneath the radar. Despite their subtle approach, these units play a remarkably decisive role in warfare.

The heavenly language comprises not just our words and sentences (verbal language) but also our body language, tone of voice, and all the deliberate and unintentional messages we communicate to others (non-verbal language).

This chapter doesn't aim to give you lessons on how to deliver a speech or how to best utilize body language. Simply acquiring such information doesn't necessarily make us better influencers; in fact, attempting to apply it might lead to confusion. Our objective is to focus on the most practical and beneficial aspects of language that will enable us to effectively influence people.

'Heavenly Language' will help us effectively convey our message by achieving the following:

1. Capturing people's attention, ensuring they are focused without any distractions;

2. Eliciting a tangible and vivid perception in people's minds, making them see, feel, and imagine our arguments, creating a distinct mental image or a scenario of our intentions;

3. Imprinting our messages in people's minds leaves a lasting impression over time, making it impossible to disregard both us and our message.

If our audience is not entirely focused on us but, instead, is distracted by the surrounding noises, our ability to influence them may be compromised. When there's a distraction, the effectiveness of our message becomes irrelevant, regardless of what we say.

If our audience cannot envision the content of our words or experience any emotional resonance, influencing them becomes challenging, even with the most compelling arguments. Unless our message is absorbed and etched profoundly in the individual's mind, they will dissipate swiftly, fading away as if they never existed.

People often listen to what we have to say out of

respect, duty, or curiosity, but our crucial messages may not genuinely penetrate their hearts. The words we express may enter one ear and swiftly exit the other, leaving no lasting impression or impact on them.

The modern world is filled with countless distractions, akin to a continuous swarm of bees buzzing loudly around us throughout the day, hindering our ability to rest or focus on any specific task. Consequently, a boring message lacking any emotional depth or visual presentation will less likely influence people.

The Power of Simplicity

People often fail to recognize that, in the realm of persuasion, they are interacting with human beings who have beating hearts. Unfortunately, they employ distant, lofty, complex, and cold language, as if they were in a graveyard attempting to convince the deceased to come back to life.

To inspire people to take action, the importance of the words we choose and the sentences we use cannot be overstated. A solitary, disparaging word delivered with disdain holds the potential to shift our mood, evoke instant tears, make us feel depressed or even physically ill. On the contrary, a supportive and uplifting word, conveyed with gentle eyes and a kind smile when we're feeling low, can elevate our spirits and kindle the spark necessary to spur us into action. Words wield extraordinary power, and are capable of shaping reality and influencing not just our destiny, but also that of others.

A close friend of mine was urgently hospitalized after

doctors discovered a severe illness during a routine examination. During my hospital visit, my friend confessed that he was afraid. This was the first time in his life that he found himself in a state of such uncertainty, devoid of any control over the unfolding events in his life.

My friend was aware of his challenging medical condition, recognizing that many people in similar circumstances had not survived this illness. Following the surgery and some time in the recovery room, the doctor entered his room holding a folder with the test results and flashing a smile. The doctor expressed that, thanks to the early detection of the disease and the successful operation, his medical condition was improving. After making a full recovery, my friend confided that what had instilled hope and a steadfast sense of resilience in him was the uplifting words from the senior doctor following the surgery.

Consider the potential outcome if, after the operation, the senior doctor had entered my friend's room with a solemn expression on his face and expressed the 'realistic' odds of surviving the disease. It is uncertain whether, in that state of mind, my friend would have been able to overcome the illness and return to us as he did.

As an attorney, I find myself questioning why lawyers, whose primary responsibility is to influence and attain outcomes, often make the mistake of using 'professional' detached and abstract language. They speak in a monotonous, mechanical manner, lacking any physical engagement, addressing the judge as if they were speaking to a doll.

The use of lofty, foreign, and complex words, with the aim of appearing wise, ironically fosters distance, arrogance, and a lack of clarity between people. Such words fail to create a genuine connection, drive people into taking action, or evoke an inspiring, vivid mental image. Simple and clear language is far more impactful than confusing messages. Keep in mind that people respond more favorably to ideas that are easy for them to visualize, making it simpler for them to recall and apply these ideas when needed.

Professor Daniel Oppenheimer carried out a fascinating study to examine people's perceptions of the use of sophisticated vocabulary as opposed to straightforward language. As part of the study, he handed out university admission forms, using three types of forms. The initial form featured straightforward words, the second incorporated intricate phrases, and the third used even more sophisticated and complex language.

Eventually, the results proved that the simpler the words, the higher the admission rate.

To master the art of influence and persuasion, we should use simple, comprehensible, and imaginative language. These elements help paint a vivid picture in the mind of the other, evoking emotions that can drive them to take action. Conversely, we will pass on abstract or complicated descriptions.

Energetic, Animated Language

Certain words possess greater weight and emotional resonance, as they evoke clear, vivid, and colorful images in our minds. Consider a sports broadcaster describing Barcelona's soccer team triumphing over Real Madrid, with Messi scoring three goals. Rather than a simple statement like "Messi defeated Real Madrid," the broadcaster would craft a more vibrant and captivating narrative for the viewers.

While the statement accurately recounts the events on the field, it's quite cold and factual and cannot evoke powerful emotions in the viewers.

Alternatively, the broadcaster can use descriptive words that will hype the crowd, such as "Messi outplayed Real Madrid" or "Messi ruthlessly dominated against Real Madrid." Words like 'overcoming,' 'trampling,' or 'crushing' the rival team, create a vivid image, as opposed to the boring term "victorious."

When the sports broadcaster talks about Messi 'dominating against' the Real Madrid soccer team, listeners instinctively visualize Messi charging through the field, much like a police car racing after a fleeing suspect.

These vivid mental images evoke stronger emotions about the situation. By enriching our vocabulary with powerful and exciting words, we can effectively inspire more people to take action.

There was a study in which 300 participants watched a video featuring a speeding car that collided with a tree. The participants were divided into two groups. One group was tasked with watching the video and answering the question: "At what speed did the car collide with a tree?" while the other group had to respond to the question: "At what speed did the car make contact with the tree?" The group that was presented with the term 'collided' in the question reported an average speed of thirty km/h higher than the responses from the second group.

That minor difference in language — 'collide' as opposed to 'make contact with' — altered the way in which people evaluated the situation. Each word paints a different image in our minds and ignites varying levels of emotion. For that reason, we should take the time to think about the words we select.

For many Jews, the term 'selection' carries significant weight as it invokes memories of the Holocaust, a time when Jews underwent a process of selection. This is important to consider. Because even if we use a word in entirely unrelated contexts, its emotional resonance persists. For example, if news reports suggest that bars in New York are discriminating against partygoers based on their skin color, it might provoke anger, though, to a lesser extent than if a broadcaster explicitly states, "New York's nightclubs engage in selection between dark-skinned and white individuals who seek to gain entrance." In the latter statement, the use of the term 'selection' would sound harmful to Jews, sparking memories of the Holocaust.

I recently watched a news program in which the host interviewed a feminist activist regarding women's rights to serve in combat roles in the military. Seated beside her was a man who opposed women's participation in combat service, asserting that they should exclusively engage in civilian service instead. The activist discussed the rights of women to serve in different roles and the significant value that stems from such service. However, in the midst of the debate, the opposing individual abruptly cut through her words.

Upon realizing that she had been interrupted mid-sentence, the activist shot the man a disdainful glance and said: "Excuse me, sir, it's my turn to speak. I didn't disrupt you, so please don't interrupt me. Don't force yourself on me. Treat women with respect." The people in the studio were momentarily taken aback by the sharp response and the words used when implying sexual harassment or 'forcing one's self on the other.'

A choice of words have transformed barbers into 'hair stylists;' the underappreciated sports teacher at school into the 'physical education teacher;' stewardesses into 'flight attendants;' and cooks in into 'chefs.'

Regaining Our Focus

Nowadays, numerous distractions surround us, splintering our attention in various directions like fragments of a wave crashing on rocks by the sea. Human attention spans are conspicuously limited and progressively diminishing. Regardless of the person with whom we are conversing, our focus inevitably wanes within moments and our thoughts drift to other matters. How can we regain our focus?

It appears that certain words have the power to draw people in. For example, words such as 'free,' 'discount,' 'sale,' or 'clearance;' these can effectively recapture the person's attention. Similarly, when discussing my child's school achievements, if her attention starts to drift, using words like "surprise" or "allowance" can snap her back into our conversation.

Another example: at the office, just before the week concludes, if the boss wants to get his employees on board with what's being said at the meeting, he should introduce words like, 'incentive,' 'bonus,' 'trip,' or 'vacation.' These words will instantly draw them in. The more relevant the words seem to the listener, the more likely they are to actively engage in listening.

When speaking to lawyers, I will incorporate words that are specifically relevant to their field in order to grab their attention. The moment I mention terms like 'attorney,' 'judiciary' or 'judgment,' their attentiveness will likely increase.

Even stating something entirely unexpected can capture people's attention. For instance, if I open a lecture in the following way: "Greetings to all the lawyers attending this lecture. One of the conclusions I reached early on in my entrepreneurial journey was... that all lawyers are thieves," I can assure you that everyone in the audience will swiftly set aside their phones and fix their gaze on me. Their attention will be focused on understanding the meaning behind the startling statement I just made.

Following a brief moment of silence, I will proceed: "That's what I thought until I became one myself. I then learned that the overwhelming majority of lawyers are actually messengers of the truth. You all deserve a round of applause." At this point, the entire audience will applaud, generating a warm and vibrant energy within the room.

Research indicates that the sound people most enjoy hearing is the sound of their own name. Politicians who appear on television frequently employ the interviewer's first name to foster a sense of camaraderie and capture attention, as in the example: "David, I will explain why your question is not relevant to our case."

Using people's first names during interviews serves as a form of flattery, albeit a subtle one, that is generally well-received. If done in moderation, this tactic has the potential to capture their attention and foster intimacy between the parties involved. Recognizing that people's concentration tends to dwindle during conversations, especially when we seek to influence them, is crucial. In the battle for attention, it is imperative to employ tactics that are engaging, interesting, and occasionally unconventional to ensure we stay in the spotlight. We'll do so by using lively, interesting words, accentuated gestures, and a distinctive tone of voice. This way, we will effectively draw attention back to us and convey our message more compellingly.

A Smart Choice of Words

What qualities do leaders possess that empower them to reshape reality and ignite revolutions? Leaders demonstrate the ability to craft impactful speeches and skillfully manipulate words to evoke emotions, instill motivation, and kindle a fervent desire to achieve goals and drive transformative changes in the world.

Words have the ability to influence our emotions. As a result, they impact our actions, shape our entire lives, and determine our destinies. The language we choose becomes an integral part of our essence, serving as a remarkable and swift tool to reshape, not only our own reality, but also that of others. In one of his most iconic speeches, Dr. Martin Luther King, Jr. declared: "I have a dream that one day this nation will rise up and live out the true meaning of its creed. We hold these truths to be self-evident that all men are created equal." These words stirred the hearts of people and instilled a profound faith that later fueled a revolution.

We, too, can harness the power of words in order to inspire, cultivate hope, and motivate people to take action.

A bad choice of words may lead to aversion or indifference, while choosing them wisely can elicit cooperation. Rather than uttering words out of habit, let us be mindful of the power we have when we speak. We should strive to broaden our vocabulary and identify words that articulate our ideas and messages most effectively.

When describing an experience, one can use the words 'amazing' or 'wonderful,' or label them as merely 'okay.' The energy and enthusiasm about the experience diminishes significantly when using the latter.

A shift in our vocabulary can alter not only how we perceive ourselves, but also how others think, feel, and respond.

Consider a scenario where a friend unexpectedly visits your office and suggests going out to lunch together. The way in which you reject their offer can make a huge difference.

For example:
- "I'm busy with work."
- "I'm under a lot of stress at work."
- "I'm overwhelmed with the amount of work I have."

Each sentence carries a distinct emotional nuance.

When meeting up with friends at a café, your response to the question, "How are you?" can significantly impact the conversation. Choosing 'great' over 'fine' signals a better mood.

Using words such as 'a little,' 'only,' or 'just' allows us to temper and diminish the emotional intensity of each experience. For instance, if I am upset with an employee for repeatedly arriving late and I wish to convey my displeasure, I might choose to moderate my tone, calling him to my office and expressing that I'm a bit frustrated with him.

The term 'fear' is more emotionally charged compared to the milder emotional value associated with words like 'discomforted' or 'concerned.'

"It's natural to feel wary\apprehensive when purchasing your first apartment, but it is the smartest decision to take in your situation because..." Surely, the word 'uncomfortable' is a better choice, as it eases the stress involved in buying an apartment.

Likewise, the word 'problem' can be reframed as a 'challenge.' "The challenges you will face after the wedding will be different from what you have experienced until now."

The term 'confusing' can become 'interesting.' "If find

the data about my business interesting" (rather than confusing).

'Disappointment' can be reframed as a 'shift in expectations.' "Parting ways with my business partner marked a shift in expectations. Time for a new journey."

Life-changing Metaphors

In one of my courtroom hearings, as I paid close attention to how the opposing lawyer spoke before the judge, I found their presentation to be exceedingly convincing. Later that day, on my way to the car, I reflected on what had led me to be persuaded by the lawyer's arguments. I recognized that he frequently employed vivid imagery and metaphors, creating a lively experience that allowed everyone to envision and feel the arguments as if they were part of a movie.

The attorney characterized the defendant as "a well-oiled machine that produces deceitful actions." Instantly, everyone in the courtroom began envisioning an intricate well-oiled machine, resembling those in military factories, churning out deceptive actions at a rapid pace. The lawyer asserted that, "the numerous damages inflicted upon the defendant now choke him like a noose tightening around the neck of someone who is about to be executed by hanging." It's nearly impossible not to visualize the defendant sentenced to be hanged in the town square. The lawyer enriched his arguments and explanations with vivid imagery and words, all the while ensuring that everyone understood what he was trying to convey.

For instance, if I need to walk a client through the challenges of handling their taxes and reducing tax payments, I might say: "Negotiating with the tax authority on your own is like talking to a brick and expecting it to respond." This metaphor helps the client understand the challenges they will face, and the reason why they should hire the help of an attorney. A metaphor doesn't rely explicitly on words such as 'like' or similar to.'

For instance:
- "I am a river that overflows whenever my wife smiles at me."
- "Our company is at the forefront of the technology industry."

Metaphors and imagery serve as powerful tools for bringing clarity to complex and we use them to imprint a vivid image in people's minds.

Visual representations leave a more profound impact than written words. For instance, an photo of someone we cherish impacts us more than simply encountering their name on a page.

The strength of metaphors and imagery lies in their ability to function as symbols, transforming into vivid emotional images. By bypassing the analytical and rational aspects of the brain, metaphors and imagery strike deep into the listener's subconscious.

I can start my lecture in the following way: "Life resembles a jungle. You've got the lion, the king of the beasts, and then there's everyone else, which basically serves as its food. Which of these do you picture yourself as?" By starting with this analogy, I encourage each individual in the audience to envision a scene or scenario unique to them. For every person seated in the audience, the jungle represents something a bit distinct.

Every person holds their own mental image of the lion feasting on all the other animals for breakfast. This mental picture will linger in their minds even after the lecture concludes. If I were to open the presentation with a statement such as, "There are those who achieve success and those who don't. Which group do you aspire to be part of?" Using this conventional opening, I may not necessarily evoke a compelling image that will resonate with the audience over an extended period.

There are two primary methods to enrich our use of metaphors and imagery.

The first one is by forming a collection of metaphors and imagery for occasions we can foresee, such as a presentation, a courtroom discussion, or sales conversations with clients.

The second method entails assembling a storage of metaphors and imagery. Whenever we encounter a captivating metaphor, we'll record it in a journal. In our free time, we will revisit this collection, reviewing all the imagery and metaphors we've gathered and assimilate them into our conversations. Over time, we will amass an impressive amount of imagery and metaphors that can be consistently employed in our interactions with others.

Let's say I'm having a conversation with my 15-year-old son about self-esteem, a valuable characteristic in life. To prepare for this important conversation, I will create a map of metaphors and imagery to better explain the power inherent in self-esteem. I'll take a paper and write the words self-esteem in the center of the page, surrounding this term with a circle. I will then answer questions and, from each response, I'll draw a line stemming from the circle of 'self-esteem.' The numerous answers will assist me in generating a substantial amount of imagery and metaphors for the conversation.

Examples of questions could include:
- What does self-esteem resemble?
- Self-esteem can unlock the door to...
- Self-esteem will dismantle barriers of...
- Self-esteem will shape...
- Self-esteem will demolish...
- Self-esteem is analogous to...

The questions and subsequent answers will help us develop more and more metaphors to employ during the conversation with the teenager to enhance his self-esteem.

We won't limit ourselves to a single answer; instead, we'll jot down a minimum of five answers for each question. It's essential, especially in the initial phase of formulating the responses, to input every answer that comes to mind without excluding those that might appear silly or irrelevant. Permitting the mind to generate every conceivable answer is vital to avoid hindering the creative process of crafting the map.

After adding enough metaphors and imagery into the map, I will select the responses that appear most fitting for my discussion. For instance, I will document the answers to self-esteem-related questions in the following way:

What does self-esteem resemble? Self-esteem is like a suit of strong armor, a brigade of well-trained soldiers advocating for you, a proficient and well-equipped tank, a key capable of unlocking any closed door in life, a guiding beacon in times of darkness, and a clear roadmap to exit an intricate maze, a water purifier, a life-saving device, a compass, a map.

Self-Esteem can open doors to … happiness, autonomy, a joyful life, memorable moments, a brighter future, better opportunities.

Self-esteem will bring down the barriers of … fear, rough times, challenges, and doubts.

Taking the child for a stroll is ideal, where I can explain him that nurturing confidence will make him feel protected, as if a sturdy steel shield is guiding him through the diverse challenges of life. I'll emphasize that self-confidence serves as a magical key, opening every closed gate and door along his life's journey. The self-esteem he develops will dispel uncertainties in his personal life and eliminate any oppressive thoughts he may have.

The metaphors I incorporate in my conversation with the child will deepen his understanding of my message, enabling him to develop additional doses of self-confidence.

In the courtroom, a lawyer can use metaphors and imagery to reinforce many points in their arguments.

For example:

- "The Supreme Court's ruling opens the door to a constructive pathway, guiding us through to the principles of human freedom."
- "The assertions in the legal claim will crumble, much like a house of cards, upon scrutiny of the defense."
- "The testimony provided by the plaintiff was served sharp as a knife, slicing the defense's claims into bits."

One can formulate a metaphorical map and align it with the theme of the lecture:

- "The lecture's topic will infuse you with the right energy to handle your business effectively."

Or, concerning the individuals you'll address in the lecture: "David Cohen, author of the book 'Recycle Your Bottles,' is the Albert Einstein of ecology."

You can also establish a metaphorical guide for the sources you incorporate:

- "Richard Guild's book stands as the bible of nutrition."
- "Robert Malone is a walking encyclopedia on human rights."

Avoid excessive use of imagery. Apply them carefully, as you would add salt when preparing a dish. An overabundance of metaphors and imagery can exhaust the audience, potentially casting us as overly poetic.

Furthermore, we should adjust the metaphors we use to suit our audience. When bringing up the topic of confidence with my 15-year-old son, it's better to avoid stating, "Your self-confidence will function like an M16 rifle on the battlefield," as this imagery may have less impact on a teenager, who normally spends his time hanging out with friends at the soccer field, as opposed to a battlefield.

When talking about self-confidence with an eight-year-old, it's best to step into their imaginative world and express, for instance, "Imagine self-confidence as a magical elixir that transforms you into a strong and powerful creature like the Hulk."

Examples of metaphors encompass standing on the edge of an abyss, demolishing barriers, teetering on the brink of mental explosion, reaching a crossroads, navigating a sea of work, feeling as free as a bird, confronting a path with no exit, shouldering the weight of the world, viewing life as a bowl of cherries, and acknowledging life as a paradise.

To shape our own paradise, we should infuse our language with vital, high-quality metaphors, while making sure not to overdo it.

When Our Words Fall on Deaf Ears

In many cases, we will follow the guidelines and employ the most sophisticated tactics of persuasion but, still, our efforts may fall short because the other party doesn't understand our choice of terminology. We may passionately explain things, and while our listeners may nod in agreement, beneath the surface, our argument may remain unclear to them.

During my training period, I was assigned the task of writing a legal complaint for one of the firm's clients. After spending hours listening to the client's story, I prepared the written claim with confidence. Upon presenting it to my mentor for feedback, I was surprised to learn that the claim I had prepared had several pitfalls. My mentor explained that, despite my in-depth understanding of the client's story, I made the mistaken assumption that the judge shared the same level of familiarity. As a result, the claim came out wordy and lacked clarity, as I used terms that the judge wouldn't necessarily understand.

My mentor shared a valuable tip with me: "Tomer, whenever you write a court request, act as if the judge reading it is a 10-year-old with zero knowledge about the field. Write in a straightforward, clear manner. Present the client's story methodically and exclude unnecessary information. Never assume that the judge is familiar with the client's world."

To this day, every time I write a court request, I ask myself whether the 10-year-old judge would be able to understand it.

Many times, people possess an abundance of knowledge in their respective fields, but when they need to transmit this knowledge to someone who lacks expertise, they fail to do so effectively. Due to a lack of awareness, these individuals often unintentionally utilize terminology and concepts that are clear to them, but obscure to their audience.

When we aim to explain something to someone, we need to tap into their existing knowledge. In that way, we can shine a light on our concepts by using metaphors or examples they'll understand. We can effectively communicate our new idea by connecting it with their pre-existing concepts and understanding.

Consider, for instance, if your 8-year-old daughter asks you, "Dad, what is electricity?" How do you even start explaining the concept of electricity to a third-grader with zero knowledge of the relevant terms? Using technical terms like volts, amps, and resistance may prove challenging, as she may not truly grasp the explanation. In fact, even when we use these terms to explain electricity to adults, many may still struggle to comprehend its true nature. Try explaining the concept of electricity through a drawing and saying, "Have you observed how water flows in a pipe? That's how electricity operates. Picture an obstacle in the water pipe, like a dam in a river, slowing down the water flow. Similarly, this is how resistance works when electricity flows." In this manner, we've conveyed a concept to the child using terms she is familiar with, bridging the gap between unfamiliar and familiar realms of understanding.

When influencing people, we should start with the assumption that they have minimal knowledge about the topic we are addressing. We will articulate our arguments and explanations as if we are addressing a 10-year-old.

We'll explain one step at a time until they fully understand. We'll use clear language to explain our ideas, using concepts and examples they can relate to in order to avoid confusion. However, we should also avoid getting too detailed or making things overly complicated, as it might make our message boring and hard to understand.

Keeping Things Clear and Concise

People erroneously believe that, by sharing all their knowledge, they can effectively persuade others. This is a common mistake that we all make from time to time. We often assume that if our conversation partner were aware of specific statistics or if we presented the bigger picture, only then could we fully convince them. The inclination to share all our knowledge with others may seem rational, yet it is fundamentally flawed. There is a belief that the more information our audience possesses, the better they will comprehend our perspective, leading to a shift in their decision accordingly.

However, most of us are sick of the repetitive babble and nonsense of those who seek to overwhelm us in order to get us on board. When I come across such individuals, I make every effort to maintain my composure, aiming to put an end to their ceaseless chatter. I've observed editors, salespeople, parents, friends, politicians, and various associates who mistreat their conversational partners by overwhelming them with a perplexing and draining barrage of knowledge and arguments. Rather than simplifying matters, an attorney tends to elaborate endlessly without providing crucial details about how they are actually going to handle the case. Undoubtedly, a few impactful sentences can seal the deal much more effectively than continuous chatter.

We appreciate those who deliver a brief, straightforward message. We admire educators, lawyers, and salespeople who organize information effectively and clearly communicate their expectations. When things appear well-ordered and balanced, it brings a sense of comfort and happiness, making us more receptive to others' communication.

When seeking to influence people, it's best to concentrate on one or two core ideas, discuss them in a concise and focused manner, and refrain from dispersing into an excess of ideas and exhaustive explanations. An adept lawyer can encapsulate the story of his client, spanning two decades and involving numerous documents within a single minute, articulating the central idea or argument in the case. Each person should be capable of distilling their message, argument, or idea clearly and succinctly from all the material and information at their disposal.

When we want to convey a message through a story, example, or analogy, it is important to ensure their relevance to our persuasive message. Otherwise, we risk confusing the audience and steering their focus away from the intended subject. Narrating a story without delivering actual insight or advice is counterproductive.

Narrating with Our Body Language
People often believe they communicate their messages exclusively through words, a thought that seems quite reasonable. After all, humans are the only beings that employ words for communication.

Although words hold a significant role, body language undeniably stands as another pivotal tool in our communicative arsenal. When trying to tell a friend you love them with an angry expression, there's a high chance they won't believe you. Therefore, it is crucial to master our bodily expressions effectively to enhance our influence on others.

In this chapter, I won't explore all the theories associated with the theory of body language or look into the meaning of every movement and gesture. I have discussed some principles in previous chapters, but the majority of these principles are challenging to apply.

In this chapter, I will concentrate on a few techniques and principles for utilizing body language. These strategies will assist in capturing people's attention and concentration, allowing us to effectively communicate our message and engage others persuasively and convincingly. As the saying goes, "A jack of all trades is a master of none" — having an excess of principles, methods, and philosophies in body language can lead to confusion, hindering our ability to apply them effectively during pivotal moments in our lives.

The guidelines presented in this chapter aim to ensure that individuals remain attentive to us and the message we are delivering, steering clear of any distractions.

The Power of Hands: The significance of hand gestures cannot be overlooked. When I look at inexperienced lawyers in court, a considerable number of them seem clueless about how to position their hands while addressing the judge. For many, hands are viewed as a bothersome distraction that needs to be dealt with, like a fly landing on our nose. They may resort to placing their hands in pockets, behind their backs, on their stomach, or at their sides, unaware that hands play a pivotal role in our overall presentation.

A straightforward model can help us understand body language. Envision a square, where its upper line begins below the chin and the lower line concludes above the belt. The two lateral lines of the square encompass the abdomen and chest. This conceptual square serves as a guide for the preferred boundary within which we should predominantly employ hand movements when engaging in communication with others, accounting for roughly seventy percent of the time.

When delivering our message, we'll aspire to have our hands move within this imaginary square. As our hands articulate and exemplify the words within the boundaries of this figurative square, people will be more likely to concentrate on us because we appear dynamic and not confined in a static, statue-like pose. Inside this imaginary square, we signal to others that we are in a state of emotional stability and comfort, confidently delivering our message. Conversely, when our hands remain stationary, either clasped or concealed in pockets, we project a sense of insecurity and disinterest. If our hands are active, spending the majority of time outside the conceptual square, it may convey emotional instability or an excess of drama.

In conversation, the impact of our words is greatly enhanced when accompanied by effective body language. By using our hands to emphasize our words, our message will resonate more effectively.

This dual processing — verbal and non-verbal — creates a powerful and tangible connection, ensuring that our message is firmly ingrained in the minds of our listeners. For example, illustrating the three benefits of our product, syncing our speech tone with the word 'three' while simultaneously signaling it with three fingers amplifies the effectiveness of our communication with the customer.

The Triangle — In the initial stages, especially when we're not yet proficient in expressing ourselves through body language, it is recommended to make extensive use of the 'triangular gesture' within the confines of our imaginary square.

This gesture should be the starting point when initiating conversations, speeches, or dialogues with others. It becomes a reliable reference to return to whenever we are uncertain about hand movements or find ourselves under pressure. In the triangular gesture, each finger on one hand touches its counterpart on the other hand, creating a triangular space between them.

The 'triangular gesture' is not just a simple movement; it is also a positive expression that communicates our belief and confidence in the message we are delivering. Consider a scenario where we are presenting to an audience and feel the initial pressure, unsure of what to do with our hands. Without overthinking, we can employ the triangular gesture to convey assurance in our message. With our hands forming the triangular shape, we have the flexibility to incorporate additional gestures, such as pointing to slides or making specific markings with our fingers, enhancing the impact of our message. If we ever find ourselves uncertain about hand movements during the conversation, we can easily revert to the triangular gesture until we identify a fitting movement that complements our message.

When we sense that our hands need more activity or we are unsure of how to use them in a conversation, introducing the triangular gestures will serve as a starting point. Gradually, we can transition from this gesture to other hand movements relevant to our persuasive dialogue.

Implementing the triangular gesture is both straightforward and influential. It is crucial to view it as the initial phase in developing compelling hand movements for effective message delivery. Through consistent practice and diversification of our body language and hand gestures, we will build confidence in utilizing body language to emphasize our message with finesse.

Narrating With Our Voices

The tone of voice accompanying our words is a remarkable tool that we should learn to use effectively. Considering the investments made by the world's largest companies in radio advertisements, it appears that the voice is an exceptionally powerful instrument for motivating people. The sound emerging from our throat is the melody of our essence.

To gain a deeper understanding of someone, pay attention to the sounds they produce when speaking; concentrate solely on the tone and disregard the words. Listen to the voices of your clients, partners, and children, as well as your boss, friends, and politicians.

Don't focus on their words or outward appearance, but rather on the sound emerging from their mouths, and you'll uncover aspects about them that were previously unknown to you.

I know several attorneys who, the moment they start speaking to the judge, turn the courtroom into a lifeless chamber. Their arguments seem uninspired and devoid of energy. In those instances, I can't help but wish I had a good bottle of wine to loosen them up a bit and inject some life back into the proceedings. Unfortunately, this style of communication isn't confined to lawyers. Regrettably, a significant number of people speak with a monotonous voice lacking passion.

The message I want to express should be clear: we should avoid succumbing to the traps of monotony and boredom. It is crucial to be mindful of the tones we emit from our mouths and breathe life into our voices, recognizing that our tone of voice serves as a potent tool to dispel boredom.

Through a deliberate and conscious use of our voices, we can attain essential objectives in effectively communicating our messages to others.

For instance:
- Attracting attention.
- Making others concentrate solely on us.
- Embedding our message more strongly in the other person's mind.
- Authentically communicating our emotions to others, establishing trustworthiness.

Our voice serves as a precise expression of the emotions churning within us. Effective leaders convey their messages persuasively by skillfully utilizing their voices to articulate emotions. In contrast, individuals lacking vitality and enthusiasm often express themselves with a monotonous and uninspiring voice.

I suggest embarking on an exploration of the remarkable and distinctive tool that is our voice, integrating it into our messages. Seek out a quiet corner where you can be alone and without distraction, whether it's in your room, in the car, or surrounded by nature. Begin experimenting with your voice. For those of you who aren't used to it, playing and training with your voice may initially feel awkward. However, over time, you'll uncover an incredible and untapped ability within yourself. In your solo training sessions, the specific words or sentences you utter are not crucial; what matters is expressing them through your voice in various forms and possible ways.

Vary your vocal expression by oscillating between loud and soft tones, fluctuate between high and low pitches, slow and fast, take brief pauses to embrace the ensuing silence and acknowledge its power. Adjust the modulation of your voice by raising and lowering it, mimic different people and animals. If the urge to laugh arises, embrace it wholeheartedly. Experiment with both yelling and whispering, infuse your sentences with a spectrum of emotions, including anger, joy, sorrow, disappointment, love, compassion, and hope. Maintain a continuous diversification of your vocal tones.

When acquiring any new skill, the initial practice might feel a bit forced and mechanical. But after several rounds of training, you will gradually gain control over your voice.

In legal settings, there are moments where the judge poses critical questions related to the case. In such situations, responding hastily and automatically is generally ill-advised. It is often more effective to pause for a brief moment, contemplating the answer until a subtle tension fills the courtroom. This approach allows everyone, including the judge, to eagerly anticipate your response, and the momentary pause empowers you to control the timing and rhythm of your answer. Although the judge initiates the exchange by asking the question, you can regain control by choosing to momentarily withhold your response.

Likewise, in serious discussions with my children, I employ the 'Silence Technique' to underscore my message. At strategic or impactful points in the conversation, I intentionally remain silent for a few moments, creating anticipation for the next words. During this pause, I reflect on my response and, when a sense of tension arises, I deliver my answer, prompting the child to engage more earnestly in our conversation.

Acting that way shows that I'm confident in my handling of time and gets my children to pay full attention to me and the message I'm delivering.

It is important not to overdo it; extended silences during the conversation can cut things off. Balance is crucial, as there is a fine line between impactful silence and silence that might unsettle the person we are communicating with, leading to discomfort.

The diverse range in our voice serves as a reflection of a rich emotional inner world. If, despite practice and training, breaking free from monotonous and one-dimensional speech proves challenging, dedicate more time to refining your voice. If needed, work on releasing your emotions, as discussed in the earlier chapters of the book. Consider every conversation with people as a form of training and an excellent opportunity to play with speech tonality. Learn which emotions to infuse into words, which words to emphasize, when to momentarily pause the flow of speech, when to express awe through words, when to speak softly, and when to employ shouting or raising your voice.

The way we articulate words significantly contributes to their meaning. For instance, the phrase 'I love you' can be pronounced slowly, or with pauses between each word. This may come off as dull or lifeless. If these words are intended to convey love, we should deliver it with passion.

I came across a video where terrorists had a hostage recite sentences scripted in advance. The captive read out the line, "They treat me very well," yet it was challenging to believe he was genuinely being treated well, as his voice told a different story.

In essence, steer clear of monotony and dullness like old wallpaper losing its grip. Don't present the message with uniformity; rather, aim to infuse variety through your voice, making it vibrant and compelling, ensuring it won't go unnoticed easily.

Heavenly Tales

What is Your Story?

This may come as a surprise, but a skillfully crafted story can wield a greater influence on individuals than a theoretical explanation, and certainly surpass a longwinded argument. The narratives woven by religious or national leaders possess formidable power, capable of reshaping the course of history, a phenomenon we witness unfolding continually.

People have listened and told stories since the era when they dwelled in caves thousands of years ago. They lit fires with stones and used bows and arrows to hunt. At the end of each day, members of the tribe huddled around a bonfire and, beneath the star-studded heavens, the tribe's elder recounted tales of brave warriors and unforgettable triumphs on the battlefield. Each tribe member was enthralled by the elder's tales, attentively absorbing the stories as they were transmitted from one generation to the next, molding the tribe's identity. These narratives granted significance and optimism to the lives of tribe members, in spite of the hardships of the time.

The Bible, recognized as the most influential book in the world, is comprised of numerous stories that have played a significant role in shaping humanity's moral, spiritual, and cultural aspects. Whether we read a book, watch a compelling movie, laugh at a humorous joke, or feel influenced by an engaging TV advertisement, we're all susceptible to the swaying power of storytelling.

Our entire day revolves around stories, whether the ones we share with others, others share with us, or the narratives we tell ourselves. When a client seeks legal advice from me, I ask them to share with me their story from start to finish. This enables me to understand their situation better and offer more effective assistance. In the courtroom, I present the judge with my client's story. An employee might share a narrative with their boss to justify a raise. An entrepreneur shares a story with investors to garner support for their new idea. And anyone in a relationship knows that there's an abundance of stories to share.

It's important to learn how to utilize the power of storytelling effectively, both in a professional context and in our day-to-day lives. Among all the studies, courses, and lectures I've participated in throughout my life, I can always recall the stories, examples, and humor shared by the instructors, with very little retention of the strategies, tactics, or overarching concepts taught. Similarly, you are more likely to recall the primary messages, ideas, and insights presented through stories and examples, and fewer of the abstract concepts, such as "The 10 rules for..." or "The 30 ways to..." approach.

The ability to tell an engaging story that gets the message across is a fundamental capability in which we should aim to become experts.

We don't need to study hard to realize that our brains are inherently better at absorbing messages when presented through stories, examples, and analogies. When someone provides me with a complex explanation that I struggle to understand, I instinctively ask them to provide an example, to clarify the matter through a story, and everything then becomes clear in an instant.

Years ago, I met one of my colleagues, a family law attorney, at the café near the courthouse to enjoy a cup of coffee before our formal discussions began. Next to my friend were two briefcases containing large binders, neatly arranged with legal documents prepared for the hearing. I casually asked the lawyer what his hearing was about today. He seemed a bit mixed up, having trouble summarizing the details of his case into a few sentences. Eventually, he shared his story in a jumbled and scattered way, tossing out arguments and facts without clear connections. He jumped around different timelines so, by the end of our chat, I couldn't quite catch the gist of the case. When a lawyer can't boil down the content at hand into a clear and focused story, it suggests he might not fully grasp his client's situation.

Can you sum up your life story or business experience in just a minute? How about sharing your country's story or your religious beliefs in one minute or even in a single sentence? Think of the stories we tell as an interesting wrapper paper for surprises or gifts. The key is in how attention-grabbing the outer layer is — does it gets people curious and excited about what's inside? Sadly, many great ideas or messages end up in the trash just because the wrapping (the story that delivered the message) wasn't catchy enough.

Picture this scenario: you've been chosen to judge a case and, on the first day, two lawyers stand before you, determined to persuade you of their correctness. The first lawyer asserts vigorously: "Honorable Judge, the accused has never physically harmed the plaintiff nor taken any money from him throughout their partnership. Instead, it is my client who has suffered due to the plaintiff's disrespectful conduct. There is no substantiation for the unfounded allegations made by the plaintiff. The claimant breached Article 4 of the agreement and, in general, the items provided were subject to specific conditions. The strongest evidence lies in the fact that the plaintiff never once signed the contract and merely exploited the defendant's trust. Hence, my client is not indebted to the plaintiff for anything; quite the contrary, it is the plaintiff who inflicted significant harm on the defendant." This is how the attorney continues to cast accusations into the void and present fragmented narratives in an attempt to persuade the judge of his client's innocence. At this stage, no one really understands the story.

Afterward, the second lawyer gets up and shares his account: "So, Mr. Joshua Nosbaum launched a fruits and vegetables marketing business three years ago. Joshua built his venture single-handedly, with no help from anyone. After a year of sweat and toil, he successfully turned it into one of the city's most thriving businesses and expanded with ten more lucrative branches. At the pinnacle of his success, Aaron Levi, the defendant, walked into Joshua's office with a collaboration proposal. Aaron would provide a unique type of fruit, found exclusively in China, and Joshua would market this special merchandise through his branch network. Joshua agreed, paying Aaron in advance with postdated checks totaling hundreds of thousands of shekels to purchase the merchandise. When the time for delivery arrived, Aaron vanished with the checks, a significant portion of which he'd already cashed, leaving Joshua without the goods. This caused Joshua severe financial setbacks leading to the closure of two network branches and substantial losses. With no other recourse, Joshua filed this lawsuit against Aaron."

This account is far more relatable and intelligible overall.

For a story to really persuade, it must be believable, interesting and engaging, with a solid structure to fit in all the points, words, and images we've talked about.

Palace of Cards or Palace of Stones: The Power of Our Narrative

Stories set humans apart from other life forms on Earth. While some creatures may roar, howl, or chirp, only we possess the ability to weave a story. In this chapter, my aim is not to instruct on the art of storytelling. I presume that all of us have a basic understanding of it. I assume we are all aware that a story has a beginning, middle, and end, along with a plot and a protagonist. In this chapter, we will delve into several key points to ensure that our narrative is focused, purposeful, and fortified with a robust and enduring framework capable of withstanding the most formidable challenges.

Every argument or explanation can be effectively conveyed through storytelling, whether we find ourselves in a courtroom, our living room, or among friends.

In my role as a department manager in a tech company, I can walk into my boss's office and express concern about the control department's performance, attributing it to a lack of motivation. Conversely, I could paint a vivid picture for my boss by recounting a recent visit to the control department on the third floor. At 2 pm, I walked into a room where everyone was buried in their computers, looking like zombies with no expressions. When I bumped into a colleague on their way to the kitchen, I casually asked, "Why is everyone so zoned out?" They replied with a shrug, "Forget it, why does it even matter? Who cares?" So, I quickly said, "It does matter. We can't let this gloomy vibe go on. We need to take action ASAP."

Just briefly, I saw a spark of hope in his eyes, like he was considering the possibility of breathing life into this dull department and making it vibrant again, just like it used to be. "Do you really want to know? I'll tell you why this department seems stuck in a rut." Surely, you spotted the differences between both forms of speech.

When we tell a story to influence people, it's like building a palace. The strength of our story is like the materials used in construction. If it's a flimsy card structure, it might collapse at the slightest breeze, but a sturdy stone-built one will stand strong against any intruder. Our story's power works in the same way.

The main idea: Every story we tell is based on a key concept that reflects our perspective on the matter. This becomes the heart of our story, the main point we want to make. This main idea acts as the punchline or central notion that drives our persuasive goal. It can be summed up in a short paragraph of about fifteen words, packing a punch. Our main idea should be interesting, avoiding being too predictable or overly simple, and should bring in a fresh perspective that captures the audience's attention (without going overboard).

To get to our main idea, we need to consider what we really want from others. What are we trying to get from them? Before we tell our story, let's paint a clear picture for ourselves. From now on, let's think about delivering any message, argument, or explanation in the form of a story.

Picture this: We're living in an isolated town with just one exit road to the big city. The road is old and dangerous, full of bumps, potholes, twists and turns, hills, and, to make things worse, it's poorly lit. After lots of requests, we finally got invited to meet with the authorities to share our concerns about this old road that's putting the folks in our town at risk. We're hoping for a solution or, better yet, a new and safer road. We enter a conference room with a spacious table at its center, surrounded by representatives from the authorities.

Here, we can let them know how upset we are about their clear legal duty, according to municipal laws and court decisions, to take care of the residents by ensuring a new and safer road. We'll point out that the current road is risky, has not been fixed for over sixty years, and falls short of the required standards set by the Ministry of Transportation. In front of the committee, we'll walk through the laws and regulations, highlighting all the problems with the road. Our main request is simple: fix the road right away, just as the head of the authority promised in the recent elections. If not, we might have to take the legal route, something we'd rather avoid. On the flip side, we could tell our story to the authority's reps in the following way:

"A few days ago, I drove from my village to the city to bring my five-year-old daughter, Rachel, to her regular checkup with the doctor. Before heading out, I strapped her in the safety seat in the back and made sure her seatbelt was snug. Rachel mentioned the belt was a bit tight, so I double-checked to ensure it was properly fastened. The drive to the city from our village is quite nerve-wracking, almost like a ride on a rollercoaster, so I buckled up in the driver's seat too. The road is indeed challenging but, as Rachel needs medical attention, we don't really have any other choice."

"Every time I drive from the village to the big city, I can't help but feel a bit anxious. I take it slow, sticking close to the outer edges of the narrow road where two cars coming from opposite directions can barely squeeze by each other. As I approach the first sharp turn, I start wondering: What if some 17-year-old, just back from a wild party in the city, decides to drive towards me at breakneck speed? What if a driver in a rush to get home veers into my lane, even if just by a hair? There's no room for maneuvering on this narrow road full of twists and turns. I take a moment to pause my racing thoughts and glance at Rachel, who's sitting in the back seat. This whole situation feels pretty unfair to her. She's innocent in all of this. Why does every trip to the city have to involve putting her life at risk?

During another nerve-wracking drive to the city, I spotted a car heading my way. I became a bit on edge and a bunch of thoughts raced through my mind. I remembered how this road had seen five fatalities in the last five years. Every year someone loses their life here, not to mention the accidents, reported and unreported, with serious injuries. I thought to myself, statistically speaking, a young person is more likely to meet their end on this road than if they were serving in a combat unit defending the country during a war.

As you can see, Rachel and I survived this risky ride. Fortunately, there wasn't a tipsy youngster coming back from a party this time. No speeding driver zooming down the lane towards us. The gap between my car and the oncoming driver was just a few centimeters. I could easily stick my hand out and touch his car.

When will Rachel and I end up as just another statistic at the Ministry of Transportation if, God forbid, we face a tragedy? Will you, dear committee members, recall that I stood here before you, practically begging you to address the road issue? If not for me, then for my Rachel and the other kids in the community who are forced to venture into the city and risk their lives on this neglected road. I'm pleading with you."

Our plea to the committee is communicated through

a personal story featuring an innocent father and his young daughter, both residents facing a dire and daily threat to their lives, trapped without any means of escape. This narrative strategically tugs at the committee members' most sensitive emotional strings, encouraging them to assume responsibility and leverage their authority to either rejuvenate or rectify the outdated road for those residing in remote areas, distanced from the urban center.

Before we prepare our story, it's crucial to grasp its core idea. Our primary assertion is that the authorities must assume responsibility, taking action to either repair the existing road or construct a new, wider, and safer one. Hence, prior to delving into the details of our story, our fundamental premise is clear: the authority has a duty to protect all of its residents. This forms the central theme and foundation around which our narrative is built.

In a legal battle unfolding in court, a lawyer is representing a farmer who is contesting the municipality's decision to expropriate a significant portion of his land for the construction of skyscrapers and commercial spaces. The municipality's decision was hastily made, with the developer's tractors already on-site and construction underway. Presently, a legal proceeding is in progress, deliberating the municipality's decision and whether to permit the developer to proceed with building on the farmer's land. The developer has deployed a legal team with the intention of stalling the court proceedings, creating a situation where facts on the ground become challenging to reverse. In response, the farmer's attorney has urgently petitioned the court to cease construction activities in the area without further delay.

In this case, the attorney advocating for the farmer presents the following idea: the entrepreneur intentionally handles the legal proceedings at a slow pace, submitting spurious motions solely to extend the timeline and solidify facts on the ground before the court steps in to provide a judgment, resulting in unnecessary delays.

The car manufacturer of a renowned company created a series of vehicles. Following their sale to customers, a safety flaw concerning the airbags came to light. Consequently, these cars have the potential to be deadly for passengers, resulting in injuries and fatalities. It seems that the car manufacturer was aware of the flaw in the production line but chose to disregard it. This decision was based on the calculation that fixing the problem for all cars from that production line would be more costly than compensating victims and families for injuries and fatalities resulting from the defect. As legal representatives, we advocate for a widow and her two children. The father of the family lost his life in a car accident due to the malfunctioning airbag, a common issue in all cars produced on that specific assembly line. Our argument in this case can be: the manufacturer's neglect in addressing the problem could be linked to the father's untimely demise.

We will find our central argument in every story we tell, be it persuading a supervisor to increase our salary, helping our child find a job, or when aiming to sell one of our products to a customer. Following the identification of the story's theme and our objectives, we will proceed to the next phase where we will respond to a set of questions. The responses to these questions will fortify the argument/message/idea within our story:

- Why should I get what I am asking for? Why am I entitled to it?
- What facts, logical reasoning, and justifications strengthen my proposition?
- What opposing arguments might the other side raise, and how do I address them?
- What story can I tell that will effectively showcase all of my arguments?

Let's document all the responses that come to mind. Following that, we'll identify the most suitable answers and craft a compelling story.

As an example, let's retrace to the story of the father addressing the local council on the topic of a new road:

1. Why should they build a new road from my far-off town to the city just for me? Well, here are some more reasons to consider:

- I pay taxes to the municipality, just like every other citizen.
- The value of my life, as well as my family's lives are equal to any other resident in the city.
- I have the same rights as any other resident to enjoy access to modern roads.
- My well-being is important.
- It falls under the authority's responsibility to protect the residents and ensure their welfare

- The municipality made a pre-election commitment to building a new road, and we voted accordingly.
- I don't want to put myself and my family at risk.
- In the long run, payment of compensation and losses due to accidents will turn out higher than road repairs.

As such, we jot down all the thoughts as to why we deserve a new road.

Now let's lay out all the facts, arguments, logic, and justification that support our case. We'll examine how many fatalities and injuries occurred on the road in recent years, starting from when the road was built and whether it was renovated in the past, what types of defects the road has and their origins, what regulations exist regarding road construction, regulations and instructions regarding proper road lighting, who pledged to build a new road in the recent elections, what regulations and laws must comply with the citizens' safety. We'll also explore the amounts the authority paid as compensation to people who were injured or killed on the road in the last 10 years, and which locations in the country and the surroundings had damaged roads repaired.

I will write down every argument, logic, justification, or relevant data related to the current case and disclose the following facts:

- Over the past five years, there have been five fatalities on this road.
- Annually, there are three road accidents resulting in at least 10 injuries.
- The road was built six decades ago and hasn't been renewed since.

- Municipal law prohibits the authority from subjecting its residents to direct hazards.
- In the latest elections, a promise was given to reconstruct a new road.
- What will the committee members say if a disaster occurs, particularly after we informed them of the dangers.
- The road is narrow, with barely enough space for two cars to pass at the same time.
- There is no lighting along the entire road.
- There are numerous curves, inclines, and descents along most of the road that obstruct the driver's visibility.

2. What could be the authority's counterarguments?
- Insufficient budget to construct a new road.
- Not enough people use the road, so there's no financial justification for investing in safety.
- The road repair issue is under the care of a special committee that will make a decision in the future.
- The committee with authority lacks jurisdiction regarding road repairs. Approval from the National Roads Committee is required.
- Constructing a new road takes years, and it's not possible to block the only road to the community for such a long time.
- The potential damage caused to people living in the community is small compared to the significant financial expenditure for building a new road.
- There are more efficient solutions, like fixing specific points in the road or installing good lighting.

3. Next, we'll outline responses to potential counterarguments.

4. Once we gather sufficient material, we'll start crafting our narrative. I may not incorporate every idea generated but will include only what's pertinent.

Where to Begin a Story

Chronologically speaking, every story has a beginning, middle and end. This doesn't mean that the story necessarily has to start from the beginning. Oftentimes, it's more interesting to spice things up by jumping to the middle or the end.

Remember the case of the widow and her two kids who lost their father in a car accident due to a malfunction in the car's airbag? The plot of this story was that the car manufacturer was accountable for the demise.

The lawyer could have started the story by giving some background on the father — his job, when he bought the car, his mood that morning, how he got the kids ready, the separation from his wife and kids, and his usual drive to work. The narrative would then move to the middle, detailing the father's commute, his last call with his wife, and the beautiful sunny day outside. Finally, the lawyer would progress to the end, describing the moment of the accident when the father crashed into a tree, and the airbags, meant to save him, didn't deploy. The scene of the accident would be painted — the wrecked car, shattered glass, smeared blood — portraying the fiery nightmare that became this unfortunate family's reality.

Alternatively, the lawyer could kick off the story from the end, providing details of the devastating car accident first. Following that, the middle and beginning of the narrative would unravel, shedding light on the father's everyday commute and his roles as a father, husband, and employee.

The attorney might choose to begin the story from the midpoint, portraying how the father joyfully hummed along to music while the sun glistened outside his window. The lawyer can then depict his final conversation with his wife, where she reveals her pregnancy. Following this, the attorney would transition to the conclusion, narrating the dreadful car crash. Only after that, the lawyer would circle back to the beginning, illustrating the father's blissful marriage, his two children, the decision to purchase a car a month earlier, the family's warm morning routine, and the poignant moments before the father bid farewell to his loved ones and stepped into the car that ultimately led to his demise.

The key idea is that a story should grab attention, hold interest, be intriguing, and throw in some surprises, regardless of where it kicks off. The length of the story doesn't automatically make it more compelling or influential; it's all about getting the structure just right. If a story is too short or drags on, it might end up dull. If you're unsure about your story, share it with others and see how they respond.

Key Rules for an Enticing Story
The stories we tell, whether to ourselves or others, aim

to convey our message convincingly and attain the goals we've set. To maximize the story's effectiveness and impact, it should embrace as many principles outlined in this chapter as possible. These principles, most of which we've encountered in the book, are now presented in the context of the story we are narrating.

1. A story is a tool to communicate a message effectively. For a story to be impactful, it should serve our message, idea, or argument; otherwise, it might confuse our audience and lead them astray from the persuasive path we've set. Every story, example, or analogy shared in the book aims to support my message and offer you value, understanding, insights, advice, or a new perspective. If a story lacks a clear point or purpose and doesn't strengthen the message, it's best to let it go, even if it's captivating, as it could hinder rather than help in achieving the intended goal.

2. Customizing the story for our audience is essential. We must tailor the narrative to the specific group we are addressing — whether it's men, women, secular or religious individuals, children, engineers, lawyers, judges, teachers, and so on. For instance, trying to communicate with women using a story that includes offensive elements or examples from the world of football wouldn't make sense. Similarly, attempting to influence a religious person with a story that ridicules their faith is unlikely to work. A story that doesn't suit or resonate with our audience can disrupt the connection between us and have the reverse effect.

3. Enhance your story with powerful words, metaphors, vivid imagery, strong arguments, suitable body language, tone of speech, and even props if possible. Utilizing this approach will result in a compelling and effective narrative.

4. Honesty. A story that isn't believable won't have an impact on people, no matter how creative it is. We won't share overly exaggerated or dishonest stories with others because lies lack credibility, and a false story won't hold up. Someone who inflates their story in an unreasonable and disproportionate way will make it less easier to believe, even if the story is true. That's why sharing accurate details is important, as it strengthens the credibility. It's best to add details such as time, location, date, names of the people involved, and more.

If I tell you a story, for example: "Yesterday at 10 a.m., I ran into David Levi on Oakwood Street and he told me about a bank robbery," it will sound more believable than if I say, "I met someone on the street who mentioned a robbery." Being specific about details enhances the credibility of our story, and the listener will trust the time, place, and situation far more.

Expressing it this way: "On a Wednesday, a cold, February morning in 1992, I strolled on the football field at my high school in Baltimore, when suddenly..." sounds much more credible than "Once I walked on the football field, and suddenly..." Including actual details in the story makes our account more trustworthy.

5. Focus on comprehension. When we tell our story, we

should check whether a 10-year-old child can easily follow it from beginning to end. If not, we need to reconstruct and plan the story again, making it simple and easy to understand, especially since people are generally more inclined to be 'lazy' when it comes to the effort it takes to pay attention. We need to lay out our story, slowly and steadily. Unsure if your story is clear enough? Tell it to one of your younger children (or nephews/nieces) and make sure they can follow. If not, your story might need some tweaking.

6. Tell your story. When telling our story, it's better to speak 'about' the incident rather than 'of' the incident. In other words, we should recount our story in the present tense, here and now, without unnecessary introductions. For instance: "It's 1998, and I'm in the courtroom. It's my turn to present before the judge. My heart pounds, and I can't bring myself to stand up and argue for my client, suddenly..." It's less impactful to tell the story in the past tense and include unnecessary sentences like, "Dear audience, I'm going to share a story about what happened to me in school many years ago. 20 years ago, I went to school like any other day, entered the classroom, but no one was there. It felt as if something strange was going on."

Instead, it's better to narrate the story in the present tense. For example: "It's 1992, and I'm walking to school like any other day. I step into the classroom, but there's no one there. A strange sensation runs through every part of my body. Suddenly..." This approach immerses the listener in the here and now.

7. The recurring chorus of our story is like the cherry on top or the jewel in the crown. While it may appear somewhat secondary at first, it adds a magical quality to our story. The recurring chorus is charming, but it is not an indispensable part of our story (the cake will be tasty even without the cherry on the whipped cream, and the crown will retain its majesty even without the jewel).

While it's possible to manage without it, a recurring chorus will add a special charm to our story. Hence, it's essential to contemplate what could serve as the memorable line. This repeated line, woven throughout the story, guarantees that the message resonates deeply and powerfully with the listener. The recurring chorus operates like a memorable jingle in an advertisement, lodging itself in our minds as we consistently hum it without interruption.

While representing a client who sued their neighbor for stealing money, I shared my client's story with the judge and inserted the following line multiple times throughout the narrative: " The defendant who was full of greed, emptied the pocket of the man in need." This is a catchy sentence, threaded like a slogan or the catchphrase of a campaign, which I repeated throughout the proceedings until the judge started smiling at me whenever I mentioned it.

When we use a catchy phrase that also includes rhymes, we make our message more memorable. Studies have shown that rhymes are perceived as more convincing, especially if we repeat the sentence several times throughout our story. For instance, if we are addressing an audience and want to convey a message about the power of positive thoughts, our recurring chorus could be: "Grand thoughts shape fate and make it great." Repeating this sentence multiple times during the presentation will embed the message deeply in the audience's minds, making it unforgettable. At one point, we can even let the audience fill in the sentence for us: "Grand thoughts shape fate and..."

When we tell a story, it's best to put in some thought and come up with a witty catchphrase, ensuring that our message is firmly etched in the minds of our audience.

Turning Copper into Gold — Dedication and Preparation

Within the pages of this book, we embarked on a journey of self-exploration. It became clear that our inter-personal relationships hold the potential to yield wonders and miracles in our lives. The right use of language, as well as clever tactics, can work a charm when influencing people.

To master the art of persuasion, it is essential to incorporate an extra ingredient into our 'recipe' for success. This often-underestimated element holds substantial value — our commitment to thorough preparation. By carefully dedicating time and effort, we can elevate our strategies, rules, laws, and tactics.

Over the years, as I diligently observed my own influence and persuasion capabilities, I realized that proper dedication and preparation, when integrated into one's lifestyle, serve as a distinguishing factor between people who are good and people who are excellent. Dedication and preparation truly make the difference between the ordinary and the extraordinary.

Many people experience frustration and a lack of

motivation as they approach the pivotal stage where they need to prepare for their 'moment of truth.' They treat it as a burden, and refuse to practice their pitch.

The most talented people we know have invested a large amount of time in order to be called 'the best.' They didn't give up, even when times were hard. Unlike them, the ordinary layperson will often give up when things become challenging, and will opt instead to plop on the couch and watch TV.

The book you are currently reading is the fruit of countless hours of labor and dedication. I found myself seated in front of the computer, tirelessly navigating between day and night, waking up at five am to write. Whether alone in my room or strolling in the forest, I poured endless hours into refining the insights written within these pages. Despite the nagging voices in my head convincing me to relax, watch TV and zoom out, a distinct voice urged the opposite, compelling me to do whatever was needed to write this book.

Building a captivating story, presenting a persuasive argument, delivering an enthralling lecture, educating children, attaining success in one's career, managing a flourishing business, holding a satisfying job, fulfilling dreams, and essentially creating your own patch of Heaven on Earth — all demand substantial dedication and meticulous preparation. This investment serves as the ultimate gateway to the life we want.

Engaging in practice and commitment involves more than just reviewing your script; it's about finding enjoyment and uncovering new insights each time. It entails meticulous study, active discourse with your project, deep understanding, analysis, questioning, reading, contemplation, and even dreaming about it at night, until it becomes an integral part of your essence.

You can surely recall the time you learned to drive: everything seemed complex, demanding, and nearly insurmountable. However, as of now, driving has become quite automatic for you, and navigating through traffic has become second nature.

Many people often find themselves stuck at the phase where they need to prepare, invest effort, and make continuous sacrifices. It is often perceived as the most tedious and uninspiring part. But it's crucial to refine our arguments, jot them down, and rehearse them repeatedly until we're thoroughly acquainted with every facet of our argument.

Think back to the days when our parents introduced us to a new game. As kids, we could lose ourselves in it for hours, completely unaware of the passing time, mastering every maneuver of the game. I suggest approaching the process of persuasion in the same way. View the process as an enjoyable, captivating children's game.

If we want to influence people, we should initiate the process by jotting down our arguments and ideas on paper or on the computer. Once we commit our thoughts to paper, the act of writing reveals creative arguments, intriguing insights, fresh ideas, and beautiful stories that we weren't aware of before we began writing. Create a space free from bustling noises and distractions. Take time for self-reflection, honing your ideas and thoughts as if you were sharpening a knife. Being alone has the potential to bring about surprising revelations.

At times, when we finish writing, we may discover that our ideas are not as strong as we initially believed them to be. It's better to make this discovery in the comfort of our home rather than on a stage in front of an audience or in our office facing our boss. Identifying these weak points during the preparation phase is better than discovering them later when there's limited room for adjustments.

Throughout our lives we encounter significant challenges that require preparation to overcome and achieve our goals. The higher the mountain in front of us, the more ready we need to be. This means jotting down our thoughts, doing thorough prep and practice, sticking to schedules in real-time, finding some quiet moments, dressing the part, and rehearsing like it's the real deal. As the saying goes, "What is difficult in training will become easy in battle."

Mastering our art is a form of superpower. You might think salespeople, politicians, or lawyers can just talk smoothly and get what they want effortlessly. Well, that couldn't be farther from the truth. Behind every great comedian's joke are hours and hours of practice, thought and effort.

Even appearing spontaneous when talking to your boss requires a tremendous amount of preparation and commitment. A few years ago I attended a lecture and, right at the beginning of the presentation, the lecturer spontaneously told a joke and the entire audience burst into laughter. During the break I approached him, and he confessed that he had worked on the joke countless times.

When we haven't adequately prepared and dedicated sufficient time to our craft, what we can do is try and fake it. However, people who slack off rarely become successful in life; they can only go so far. People who don't put in the effort or show up unprepared might seem impressive in casual situations, where sweet-talking or bluffing is the norm. But when it comes to achieving meaningful things in life, these people stumble.

People who invest in things that matter to them are, above all, people who care about themselves and others. So, if you want to make an impact, start by genuinely caring. If you're not ready, it's a sign you might not care enough. When I truly care, I step out of my comfort zone, do whatever it takes, and put in the time needed to make dreams, whether they be mine or someone else's, come true.

In today's modern culture, people rely too much on their feelings and invest little time in putting actual thought into their actions. People prefer to take shortcuts, yet somehow expect to become experts. Only after you've already mastered your field can you enjoy the fruits of your labor. For example, a doctor with a year of experience is not the same a doctor boasting 25 years of practice.

If you're aiming for success, promise to steer clear of arguments as noisy and hollow as a soda can rolling down a paved road. Get ready, invest time in what matters to you, and watch as your life becomes a slice of Heaven on Earth.

Made in the USA
Las Vegas, NV
04 February 2025